SpringerBriefs in Applied Sciences and Technology

From the European Space Policy Institute

The books in this series cover various space-related domains including space policy and strategy, governance, space economy, space law and regulations, space diplomacy and international relations or space security among others. They aim at supporting a good understanding of the issue they cover and at providing ESPI perspectives on the topic. Each book explores an important area of space policy development and provides a comprehensive overview of the topic and an in-depth analysis of the main implications for the space sector. Information and positions provided in the reports are the result of a thorough background research including extensive literature review and key stakeholders interviews and of space policy experts analyses.

More information about this subseries at http://www.springer.com/series/15974

Marco Aliberti · Matteo Cappella ·
Tomas Hrozensky

Measuring Space Power

A Theoretical and Empirical Investigation on Europe

ESPI
European Space Policy Institute

Springer

Marco Aliberti
European Space Policy Institute
Vienna, Austria

Matteo Cappella
European Space Policy Institute
Vienna, Austria

Tomas Hrozensky
European Space Policy Institute
Vienna, Austria

ISSN 2191-530X ISSN 2191-5318 (electronic)
SpringerBriefs in Applied Sciences and Technology
ISSN 2523-8582 ISSN 2523-8590 (electronic)
SpringerBriefs from the European Space Policy Institute
ISBN 978-3-030-15753-1 ISBN 978-3-030-15754-8 (eBook)
https://doi.org/10.1007/978-3-030-15754-8

This Springer imprint is published by the registered company Springer Nature Switzerland AG
The registered company address is: Gewerbestrasse 11, 6330 Cham, Switzerland

Preface

With the dramatic increase of global space activities, references to the term space power have become exceedingly common within the general press and the academic literature alike. Despite its apparent self-explanatory nature, there is still no widely acknowledged definition of the term, let alone a comprehensive theory explaining its significance and implications.

This study devises a novel conceptual framework to analyse the concept of space power and provides key analytical tools to empirically measure and compare different typologies of space actors on the basis of well-defined criteria. This book hence identifies a comprehensive set of conditions required to reach and maintain the status of space power and investigates the major political, security and socio-economic stakes at play. Building on this, this book conducts a comparative assessment of the major space actors, the underlying aim of which is to examine Europe's relative position in space arena and put into perspective its purported ambition to assert itself as a space power with the necessary means and resources required to meet this goal.

This book will prove a valuable and versatile tool to support European decision-making and will offer key insights into executives, space professionals and scholars alike.

Vienna, Austria

Marco Aliberti
Matteo Cappella
Tomas Hrozensky

Acknowledgements

The authors would like to express sincere thanks to ESPI Director, Jean-Jacques Tortora, and ESPI Coordinator of Studies, Sebastien Moranta, for their continuous and most valuable support throughout the course of this project. More broadly, the authors wish to express great appreciation to the entire ESPI team, and in particular to Matteo Tugnoli, Annalisa Donati, Giulia Bordacchini, Mathieu Bataille and Sara Hadley, for their useful feedback, assistance and cooperation in the execution of the comparative assessments presented in this study.

The authors are furthermore grateful to all experts and stakeholders interviewed under Chatham House Rule during the preparation of this study and to the many people that reviewed it and provided constructive feedbacks. Sincere thanks are in this context extended to the members of the ESPI Advisory Council for their useful critiques as well as Jaque Grienberg, Maximilian Betmann, Victoria Samson and Rodrigo Praino for their additional and thought-provoking comments during the finalisation of the study. Finally, the authors would like to highlight the invaluable assistance offered by professor Ottorino Cappelli, whose academic research at the University of Naples "L'Orientale" provided a sound theoretical foundation for the conduct of this study and whose critical suggestions further contributed to refine its quality during the review process. Of course, it remains that responsibility for errors and infelicities now rests with the authors.

About ESPI

The European Space Policy Institute (ESPI) is an independent public think tank based in Vienna focusing on international and European space affairs.

ESPI provides decision-makers with an informed view on mid- to long-term issues relevant to Europe's space activities. In this context, ESPI acts as an independent platform for developing positions and strategies. The institute fulfils its objectives through various multidisciplinary research activities leading to the publication of books, reports, papers, articles, executive briefs, proceedings and position papers, and to the organisation of conferences and events including the annual ESPI Autumn Conference.

The institute is supported by 17 members including the Austrian Research Promotion Agency (FFG), the European Space Agency, the European Commission, national space agencies and major satellite operators and manufacturers. Located in the heart of Vienna, the centre of international space diplomacy, ESPI has developed a privileged relationship with the United Nations Office for Outer Space Affairs (UNOOSA) and with a network of space policy experts in Europe and across the globe.

More information on ESPI is available on ESPI website: www.espi.or.at

Contents

Acronyms

APRSAF	Asia-Pacific Regional Space Agency Forum
ARTES	Advanced Research in Telecommunications Systems
ATV	Automated Transfer Vehicle
BIC	Business Incubation Centre
CSDP	Common Security and Defence Policy
DARPA	Defense Advanced Research Projects Agency
DG GROW	Directorate-General for Internal Market, Industry, Entrepreneurship
EC	European Commission
ECI	European Component Initiative
ECS	European Cooperating States
EDA	European Defence Agency
EEE	Electrical, Electronic and Electromechanical *(parts, components…)*
EGNOS	European Geostationary Navigation Overlay Service
EIC	European Innovation Council
ESA	European Space Agency
ESCC	European Space Components Coordination
ESPI	European Space Policy Institute
ESTMP	European Space Technology Master Plan
ESTRACK	European Space Tracking Network
EU	European Union
EVA	Extra-Vehicular Activity
FP7	EU Seventh Framework Programme
GNSS	Global Navigation Satellite System
GOVSATCOM	Governmental Satellite Communications
GPS	Global Positioning System
GSA	European GNSS Agency
GTO	Geostationary transfer orbit
H2020	Horizon 2020

HR	High Representative for Foreign Affairs and Security Policy
ISR	Intelligence, Surveillance, Reconnaissance
ISRO	Indian Space Research Organisation
ISS	International Space Station
ITAR	International Traffic in Arms Regulations
JAXA	Japan Aerospace Exploration Agency
JTF	Joint Task Force
JTI	Joint Technology Initiative
LEO	Low Earth Orbit
MFF	Multiannual Financial Framework
MPLM	Multi-Purpose Logistics Module
NASA	National Aeronautics and Space Administration
NATO	North Atlantic Treaty Organisation
NEOs	Near-earth objects
OECD	Organisation for Economic Cooperation and Development
PESCO	Permanent Structured Cooperation
PNT	Positioning, Navigation and Timing
ROI	Return on Investment
RPO	Rendezvous and proximity operation
SME	Small and medium enterprise
SSA	Space situational awareness
SST	Space surveillance and tracking
STEM	Science, technology, engineering and mathematics
THAG	ESA Technology Harmonisation Advisory Group
TRL	Technology readiness level
TT&C	Telemetry, Tracking and Command

Chapter 1
Introduction

1.1 Background

Speaking at the 9th annual Conference on European Space Policy in January 2017, the EU High Representative for Foreign Affairs and Security Policy, Federica Mogherini, highlighted that "Europe can be and should be a space power" (European External Action Service, 2017). The High Representative also made clear that this objective was to be pursued for several political, economic and security reasons, but could be achieved only by "acting together, as a true Union".

A few months later, in her keynote speech at the Space Symposium in Colorado Springs, EU Commissioner Elżbieta Bieńkowska provided the audience with a different message. She stressed that "Europe, and many of its Nations, has always been an important space power", and that through the new European space strategy, Europe has set its "vision and ambition for space: to remain a space power and to embrace the challenges ahead" (European Commission, 2017). Interestingly, the Commissioner also argued that "with a cumulated budget of 7 billion a year, Europe [today] is the second space power in the world, and we intend to preserve and amplify this position" (Ibid.).

The apparent mismatch in the views expressed by the two EU commissioners not only underscores a possible discrepancy in the assessments of two important EU´s bodies, but more broadly raises several questions regarding the very notion and constituent elements of space power. What are the key features defining such status? Are there specific criteria to be used for differentiating a space power from a *lesser* space actor? And how can they be empirically measured and assessed? Eventually, can a hierarchy among space actors be established on the basis of these criteria?

Within the body of the space power literature these questions have not been fully answered. This is not surprising considering that debates around the meaning and nature of space power have yet to reach an agreed upon definition and conceptual framework. As of 2019, there is still no widely accepted definition of space power, let alone a comprehensive theory explaining its exact significance and implications.

M. Aliberti et al., *Measuring Space Power*,
SpringerBriefs from the European Space Policy Institute,
https://doi.org/10.1007/978-3-030-15754-8_1

Equally important, for understandable reasons the literature has focused mostly on the United States and Russia so far. More recently, interests have been aroused by China's space achievements and its openly asserted resolve to be "a space power in all respects", while European nations have been put aside individually, and always been considered instead as a whole. Europe, therefore, emerges from the literature as a complicated and intertwined tangle of relations, institutions, and national interests; a tangle that somehow still manages to be second-best in the space dominion, but which really struggles to reach the full status of space power.

This work will focus on this issue—whether Europe, through its various constituents, can be considered a space power and what the implications of its actual status and position within the international space arena are. Towards this, there is a need to define a framework to explain and analyse the concept of space power, and ultimately offer analytical instruments to examine and put into perspective European strategic ambitions and the necessary means and resources required to meet such ambitions.

1.2 Objectives and Structure of the Study

The study has a threefold objective:

- Methodically define and explain the concept of space power from both a theoretical and empirical point of view;
- Identify a comprehensive set of conditions required to reach and maintain the status of space power, and investigate the strategic, diplomatic, and socio-economic stakes at play;
- Assess Europe's space power status (or lack thereof) and the underlying implications associated with its relative position in the global space arena.

Consistent with the three identified objectives, the study is comprised of three major chapters, each focusing on one specific aspect.

Chapter 2 analyses space power from a theoretical perspective. It starts with a review of the existing definitions and theories on space power and assesses their major features and flaws. Subsequently, the chapter devises a novel framework for explaining and measuring the concept of space power by working on a clear distinction between different typologies of space actors through the utilisation of measurable criteria.

Chapter 3 has an empirical dimension and provides a comparative assessment of the major space actors worldwide on the basis of the identified sets of criteria. The chapter will more specifically compare and identify the current status of China, India, Japan, Russia, the U.S. and Europe.

Finally, Chap. 4 will provide an in-depth examination of Europe's position in the space arena. It must be immediately noted that such an investigation poses a specific analytical problem related to the appropriateness of discussing Europe as a single, distinct player within the international landscape for space activities—in other words,

Europe's *space actorness*. Europe is obviously not a nation-state in a Westphalian sense, nor is it a polity that has emerged from a single, authoritative source as in the other space nations. The European Union (EU)—which is the result of a long-standing project of integration initiated more than half a century ago and thus usually regarded as the geo-political entity representing Europe—is itself problematic by virtue of the fact that "it is something more than an intergovernmental organisation, but still less than a fully-fledged European state" (Wallace, 2005). In addition, when looking at the issue from a space perspective, the EU is neither the only nor the most directly involved actor in the management of European efforts in the field. That role has traditionally belonged to the European Space Agency (ESA).

In fact, if a European *space actorness* is to be identified, this can be said to result from the complex interplay of three distinct constituencies, which create a triangular governance structure. At one tip is ESA, an intergovernmental organisation, which over the past 40 years has taken the lead in carrying out the major European space endeavours and in strengthening the European space identity, though lacking political clout. At a second tip there is the EU, which has only recently started to position itself as an additional and effective space player, demonstrating the willingness—and in a sense the legitimacy—to complement ESA´s actions with political leadership in a few given programmatic areas. At the third tip there are the different member states of both organisations which, despite a common basis of 18 states, do not exactly coincide. Each player in this composition has its own specific competences and interests (Aliberti, 2015).

Notwithstanding the institutional divergences among the various actors, this study finds reasonable to empirically analyse Europe as a unified, though *sui generis*, space actor by taking into account all these specificities. Therefore, building on the comparative assessment provided in the second part, Chap. 4 will first explain what particular kind of actor Europe is, by clarifying why it cannot be considered a fully-fledged space power. Building on this, the chapter will then discuss whether Europe *should* become one, by disentangling the economic, political and security stakes at play. Finally, the chapter will elaborate on whether Europe *can* become a space power, by identifying the means and conditions to fulfilling this possible goal.

References

Aliberti, M. (2015). *When China goes to the Moon*. Vienna: Springer.

European Commission. (2017). *Europe: ready in Space, working together in Space*. Retrieved from European Commission: https://ec.europa.eu/commission/index_en.

European External Action Service. (2017). *EU must be a space power, says High Representative Mogherini*. Retrieved from European External Action Service: https://eeas.europa.eu/.

Wallace, W. (2005). Post-sovereign governance: The EU as a partial polity. In H. Wallace, W. Wallace, & M. A. Pollack (Eds.), *Policy-making in the European union* (pp. 483–503). Oxford: Oxford University Press.

Chapter 2
Analysing Space Power: A New Conceptual Framework

The aim of this chapter is to devise a proper framework to explain and analyse the concept of space power. Towards this, the chapter will first provide an overview of the available definitions and theories of space power, their key features as well as their major shortcomings. Second, the chapter will identify and introduce new building blocks for a more coherent, consistent and effectively measurable concept of space power, working on a clear distinction between space powers, spacefaring nations, and emerging space actors on the basis of well-defined and measurable variables and criteria. Finally, the chapter will identify and discuss the stakes associated with reaching and maintaining the status of a space power.

2.1 Introducing the Concept

Defining space power is neither a new nor an easy task. As of 2018, there is still no fixed, widely accepted definition, but rather a plethora of different and sometimes diverging definitions. Perhaps more striking is that there is no fixed taxonomy across different works and publications, as authors have been alternating *space power* with *spacepower* indistinctively, using the two terms to refer to either actors or their capabilities.

In order to support the reader, avoid confusions, and provide a certain order within the text, in this study:

- **space power** is always used when referring to an actor, be it a country or not, while
- **spacepower** will refer to the set of attributes necessary to be deemed a space power.

To maintain consistency within such self-imposed margins, when quoting third parties' works, space power and spacepower will be edited—if necessary—and consequently highlighted in *italic*.

M. Aliberti et al., *Measuring Space Power*,
SpringerBriefs from the European Space Policy Institute,
https://doi.org/10.1007/978-3-030-15754-8_2

2.1.1 *Defining Spacepower and Space Power*

Spacepower is an analytically ambiguous concept. This is not surprising given that the very role and nature of "power" remains a matter of controversy among political scientists. To quote Gray, "any concept which embraces the word "power" accepts the ambiguities of that difficult term" (Gray, 1996, p. 299). Therefore, when trying to define what spacepower is, it is necessary to make a step back and briefly clarify the concept of power.

There is wide consensus that "the concept of power is both exceedingly slippery to pin down and yet indispensable in enabling one to analyse a number of important social issues" (Blalock, 1989), including space policy and politics. In social sciences, power has been defined in several different ways, but from an overall perspective, it is possible to distinguish between two broad approaches, here referred to as "capacity-oriented approaches" and "status-oriented approaches".

- Power as an attribute includes conceptualisations focusing either on the material components of power or the relational aspects thereof. These conceptualisations encompass a variety of definitions such as the one proposed by Dahl (which defines power as A getting B to do something that B would not otherwise do) (1957), Nye ("the ability for a country to affect outcomes according to its preferences, interests, and if necessary change the behaviour of other actors in order to achieve desired outcome") (2003), Barret and Duvall ("power is the production, in and through social relations, of effects that shape the capacities of actors to determine their circumstances and fate") (2005), etc.
- Alongside these capacity-oriented definitions, political scientists and international relations scholars, have devoted much effort to determining what entities are deemed to have the "status of power" and how such status can be empirically measured on the basis of certain well-defined factors. These approaches generally tend to consider states as "resource containers" possessing certain measurable attributes and ranking order among them on the basis of such attributes (Tellis, Bially, Layne, McPherson, & Sollinger, 2000). To reach the status of a power, and therefore be considered as such, it is necessary to gain and master a certain amount of power as capacity. Those entities having a significant amount of power in military, diplomatic, cultural, and economic spheres are called "great powers", although the existing variables that should be employed to measure such power and how they relate internally remains a matter of debate.

This distinction also applies to the concept of space power (as status) and spacepower (as capacity), with a first useful definition being drawn along such duality by Lupton in his *On Space Warfare*, in 1988:

> Spacepower is the ability of a nation to exploit the space environment in pursuit of national goals and purposes and includes the entire astronautical capabilities of the nation. A nation with such capabilities is termed a space power. (Lupton, 1988, p. 4)

Lupton's definition provides a first useful insight into the discussion of what a space power is, explicitly underlining the twofold connotation of the term. Space power is therefore the status that a nation reaches once it has mastered the ability to exploit the space environment through the full spectrum of capabilities. The *astronautical capabilities* mentioned by Lupton can include a wide array of elements and means, be them assets, technologies, or know-how, related to the various branches of space activities (Earth observation, navigation, timing and positioning, satellite telecommunications, human spaceflight, space science, planetary exploration, etc.) but also wider power-related means, such as military exertion, diplomatic ability, influence, industrial flexibility, economic prowess, and so on. It is therefore clear that an actor will have to own and master each one of these elements to be considered a *space power*, and it is likewise clear that *spacepower* is peculiarly transversal in what it encompasses.

In the decade following Lupton's *On Space Warfare*, the debate on space power heated up, also as a consequence of the Gulf War, in which space assets made a real difference in combat for the first time.

A series of definitions was proposed by various authors and scholars, an overview of which is provided in A.1—List of definitions of Spacepower and Space Power. These definitions juggle various recurring elements, alternating or combining them, but the overall focus is on the "capacity" dimension of power.

To illustrate, in 1994, spacepower was defined as "the ability to exploit the civil, commercial and national security space systems and associated infrastructure in support of national security strategy" (Jusell, 1998). In 1995, Hyatt proposed considering spacepower as "the ability of a state or non-state to achieve its goals and objectives in the presence of other actors on the world stage through control and exploitation of the space environment" (Hyatt, Paul, Rampino, Ricchi, & Schwarz, 1995), while in 1996, spacepower was envisioned by Gray as "the ability to use space while denying reliable use to any foe" (Gray, 1996).

Again, between 1997 and 1998, the Air Force Doctrine Document 2-2, defined spacepower as "the capability to exploit space forces to support national security strategy and achieve national security objectives" (U.S. Air Force, 1998), becoming, one year later, "the pursuit of national objectives through the medium of space and the use of space capabilities" in the definition by Johnson, Pace and Gabbard. Relevantly, these authors also highlighted that "spacepower is connected to other forms of national power such as economic strength, scientific capabilities, and international leadership" (Johnson, Pace, & Gabbard, 1998), a relevant aspect that was more thoroughly addressed by James E. Oberg in his *Space Power Theory* (1999).

Commissioned by the U.S. Space Command and published in 1999, Oberg's work arguably represents the most complete effort in defining spacepower and space power, drafting a fully comprehensive theory for how a space power can be evaluated, how it can build capabilities, and definitely shape and apply its own spacepower. Spacepower is, in fact,

> the combination of technology, demographic, economic, industrial, military, national will, and other factors that contribute to the coercive and persuasive ability of a country to politically influence the actions of other states and other kinds of players, or to otherwise achieve national goals through space activity. (Oberg, 1999, p. 10)

This definition of spacepower is surely the widest in scope and one of the clearest available, adding to the many reasons that make Oberg's work one of the most appreciated in this field. Oberg tried to include many factors and elements contributing to a nation's spacepower, explaining why each of these is relevant, and directly implying that spacepower is not exclusively about military goals.

More recently, a definition of spacepower was provided by Lutes and Al-Rodhan, who, similar to Oberg, significantly expanded the scope of the concept, connecting spacepower to other forms of national power. More specifically, in his *Spacepower in the twenty-first Century*, Lutes states that "spacepower both contributes to and is supported by other forms of power: diplomatic, informational, military, and economic, among others" (Lutes, 2008, p. 67), while Al-Rodhan defined it as the ability to use space in function of what he calls *state capacities*, namely "social and health, domestic politics, economics, environment, science and human potential, military and security, and international diplomacy" (Al-Rodhan, 2012).

From this brief inventory of definitions, two important considerations come to the fore.

- First, the primary focus of all these definitions is on the capacity rather than status dimension of spacepower. Spacepower overall emerges as an ability to use, exploit or control the space environment to pursue and achieve national goals, including first and foremost national security objectives.
- Second, and over the years, there has been a progressive expansion in the scope of the definition, with spacepower capabilities becoming intertwined with a nation's overall infrastructure, industrial, scientific, and institutional apparatuses, rather than being simply military- and national security-oriented. As compared to earlier definitions, focusing almost exclusively on the military and national security realms, more recent definitions come with many different elements—economy, demography, industry, technology, etc.—and a wider spectrum of potential spacepower applications—pursuit of national goals, influence, persuasion, coercion—which finally hint at the all-inclusiveness of spacepower.

2.1.2 Theories on Spacepower

Drawing upon the set of available definitions, a series of diverse and sometimes diverging spacepower theories have been elaborated since the 1990s, aiming to provide both analytical tools to understand the composition of a nation's spacepower, and to guide decision-makers when setting national political and strategic directions.

As of 2018, the body of the spacepower literature still lacks a comprehensive spacepower theory but encompasses a variety of theories making use of the most diverse approaches. These range from the elaboration of warfare theories focusing on space as a medium, to broader discussions on the role of space in and enhancement of national power and the pursuit of a country's objectives, passing through traditional international relations theories, as well as analyses close to science fiction.

Trying to bring some order to the discussion, Brian E. Fredriksson has divided the existing theories into three schools of thought: the classical theorist school, where spacepower theories are somewhat extended from existing land-, sea-, and airpower theories; the categorical school, which encompasses theories trying to divide the use of space in doctrinal categories; and the propositional school, which includes theories developing around a finite number of propositions about space features and implications. (Fredriksson, 2006)

Notwithstanding this variety, the most diffused approach in the development of spacepower theories has been the comparison of spacepower to land-, sea-, and airpower, with theorists trying to find common elements between space and the other war-fighting domains, drawing lessons for the space medium from the "masters" of the past, such as warfare theorist Carl von Clausewitz, seapower theorists Alfred T. Mahan and Julian Corbett, and airpower theorist Giulio Douhet, et al.

Among the authors mentioned in Sect. 2.1.1, Gray based his work drawing upon Mahan's seapower theory, even rephrasing Mahan's *The influence of Seapower upon History* into his own *The Influence of Space Power upon History*, while John J. Klein, who considered that Mahan had fallen short in integrating space with the other three mediums, applied Corbett's work instead. Many scholars, such as for instance France (2000), Fox (2001), Wagner (2005), Harter (2006), and Klein (2006), have tried to develop a comprehensive spacepower theory drawing upon the work of previous theorists in a specific terrestrial medium, with Wagner, in his *Spacepower Theory: Lessons from the Masters* analysing land, sea, and airpower theories and describing all the various elements that could find military and strategic applications in the space medium (Wagner, 2005). For instance, Wagner applied Mahan's concept on the control of so called choke-points, stating that "spacepower must include the capability to block information and/or physical traffic to and from space", while Douhet highlighted the need to "prevent the enemy from launching and attaining orbit while retaining the ability to orbit oneself and be able to cut an enemy's army and navy and air force off".

Among all the available theories—a concise overview of which is provided in A.2—List of Spacepower theories—specific mention must be made of the efforts of Oberg in *Space Power Theory* and the theory developed by Everett C. Dolman in his *Astropolitik: Classical Geopolitics in the Space Age* (Dolman, 2001).

Oberg built on the idea that the underdeveloped level of space technology does not allow for an historical comparison with the emergence of airpower theories. Given that current space technology is more comparable to the military use of hot air balloons in the XIX century rather than post WWI air flight, Oberg argued that it is hard to design a spacepower theory (given the different stages of technologies) by comparing it with ideas from airpower or seapower theorists (Oberg, Space Power Theory, 1999, pp. 121–122). He thus developed a set of 13 *truths* and *beliefs* on spacepower, focusing on the technicalities of operating in, through, to and from space (Oberg, Space Power Theory, 1999, pp. 124–131). Among these, Oberg highlighted the existence of space as a distinct medium, the relevance of space situational awareness, and the necessity of space control as the "linchpin upon which a nation's space power depends", predicting the inevitability of the weaponization of space. He also stressed that "space power, alone, is insufficient to control the outcome of terrestrial conflict or ensure the attainment of terrestrial political objectives", underlying that for the near future space will need to be integrated to and with other means, albeit being a separate medium on its own.

Everett Dolman, conversely, drew inspiration from classical geopolitics—in particular around Sir Halford Mackinder's and Nicholas Spykman's geopolitical theories of the Heartland and the Rimland—for the development of his *Astropolitik*. With this term, the U.S. scholar referred to "the application of the prominent and refined realist vision of state competition into outer space policy, particularly the development and evolution of a legal and political regime for humanity's entry into the cosmos" (Dolman, 2001). In a similar fashion to classic geopolitical focus on geographic regions and strategic control points, Dolman portrayed a cartography of outer space, which "emphasizes orbits, regions of space, and launch points as geopolitically vital assets over which states can be expected competitively and strategically to struggle for control" (Havercroft & Duvall, 2009). In doing so, he even rephrased one of the most eminent geopolitical maxims by arguing:

> Who controls low-earth orbit controls near-Earth space. Who controls near- Earth space dominates Terra. Who dominates Terra determines the destiny of humankind. (2001, pp. 6–7)

Overall, Dolman offered "a spacepower theory that is focused almost entirely on the political rather than technical aspects of spacepower" (Hays, 2014, p. 59). Compared to Oberg, Dolman hence provided an overall vision, a political direction for a space power to follow, suggesting that the U.S. should take control of low earth orbit (LEO), and overall impede access to any adverse entity, to better exploit space and exert its spacepower.

While both Oberg and Dolman are considered to have "[opened] a new phase in the strategic understanding of space" (Gray, 2001), there is also consensus that "to date, no holistic spacepower theory has yet emerged that is fully worthy of claiming a place alongside the seminal seapower and airpower theories" (Hays, 2014). This is mainly due to the inherent flaws of these theories.

2.1.3 Some Critiques

Having briefly overviewed current spacepower and space power definitions and theories, it is now useful to point out major setbacks and flaws that these have and to try to draw some insights on how to elaborate a more useful definition/theory. In fact, four major drawbacks stand out.

2.1.3.1 Narrow Focus

For one thing, most space power theories prove to be excessively narrow-focused. Even though, to quote Lutes, "spacepower can be looked at through sociocultural, economic, and security lenses, each roughly equating to the civil-scientific, commercial, and military intelligence sector of space activity" (Lutes, 2008), theorists have so far looked at spacepower through the military/security lens, particularly doing so by exploiting the work of the "masters" of the past.

This is not surprising given that the origin of the debates around spacepower was set in the context of the Cold War and the Gulf War, with the national security and military dimensions inevitably emerging as the predominant elements of spacepower definition. However, almost two decades in the NewSpace age, it appears clear that spacepower should be analysed from a wider perspective, with theories embracing perspectives on the growing use and importance of space in areas that go beyond its military uses.

In this respect, it is worth recalling that, as early as 1999, Oberg raised a relevant point never fully addressed by following theorists. He argued that "the emergence of a commercial space industry that owns and operates a growing majority of space systems signals a maturity in space power previously lacking", adding that "any useful theory of space power must take this commercial aspect into account", given that "it will be the commercial manufacturers, owners, operators, and users who will contribute the larger, if less clearly perceptible, aspects of space power" (Oberg, Space Power Theory, 1999, p. 125). Yet, despite the general appreciation of Oberg's work, and despite the multifaceted nature of spacepower, the majority of spacepower theories have continued to be focused on the military and security related realms, ignoring the wider and more diverse connotations that *space powers* have in exerting their *spacepower*.

2.1.3.2 Improper Extrapolations

Beside their narrow, military-oriented focus, a second major flaw common to most spacepower theories is that they have been extrapolated from warfare and power theories from the past, generally recycling notions used for land, sea, and air power. This extrapolation, however, is inherently cumbersome for multiple reasons. For one thing, as Hays has pointed out, "[f]ew concepts from seapower theory translate directly into airpower theory, and it is not reasonable to expect either seapower or airpower theory to apply directly for the distinct medium of space" (Hays, 2014, p. 61).

By trying to find useful analogies between land, sea, air and space, most theories tend to overlook the uniqueness of the space medium, such as the physics involved, which makes analogies technically hard or highly unlikely due to their implications. It is for instance unclear how airpower can be compared to spacepower, since aircraft can fly in multiple directions, unnoticed, with the possibility to be refuelled, while spacecraft, conversely, follow predictable orbits, are constantly tracked, even by amateurs, and have manoeuvring capabilities constrained by orbital mechanics and—for now—limited, finite, fuel capacity. Similarly, controlling chokepoints via sea results in a quite different endeavour from controlling, for instance, a specific orbital

Table 2.1 The analogy between space and the high ground

High ground on earth	High ground in orbit
The high ground is hard to reach and build on	The high ground is extremely hard to occupy and build at
The high ground has physical resources for shielding and hiding	The high ground has zero physical resources
The high ground is a "castle on a peak", a fort on a rock—A symbol of power	Objects in the high ground are easy, vulnerable targets
The high ground provides a view of all below while concealing the viewer	An object in the high ground is visible and trackable, ground players can hide
The high ground offers an advantageous position to strike anywhere, limiting those below in reaching it	Attacks from the high ground follow predictable paths and timing, ground attacks are highly unpredictable in both
Weapons positioned on the high ground are more effective when aimed downward, attacking uphill adds difficulties and delays	Attacking uphill/downhill are similar, plus resupplying the high ground is much harder
The high ground permanently controls strategic routes and territories, and can interdict any traffic	The high ground is a slip-sliding Maginot Line, easily avoided, outwaited and circumvented

Source Oberg (2005)

plane or a Lagrange point. Indeed, the very comparison of space as the ultimate high ground can be misleading (see Table 2.1).

In addition, these comparisons do not really consider that the current costs and level of space technologies still remain a major setback for operations and activities for any actor: a space power today is certainly not operating in, through, to and from space with the same extent, scope of activities, practicality and intuition as a land, sea, or air power would in, through, to and from land, sea, or air. As Oberg pointed out, the current level of space technologies makes current spacepower only an embryonic version of what it could be in the future. It is therefore premature to build spacepower theories, which today rely only on early-stage spacepower capabilities, on seapower or airpower theories, envisioned for fully developed, functional and operational technologies. In short, by comparing space to themes that have emerged from Earth-side history, theorists eventually force analogies, shut off possible insights, and conjure up false implications—and the result can be bad choices and policies (Oberg, 2005).

In the final analysis, if one wishes to learn from previous power theorists, one should consider airpower advocate William Mitchell, who suggested that the development of an airpower theory required new rules and ideas of strategy (Wagner, 2005, p. 20–24). Indeed, when applying this to space, it can be argued that the development of a spacepower theory would need the same novelty introduced by airpower, rather than an adaptation of previous theories, which would reflect naivety rather than novelty.

2.1.3.3 Impractical Propositions

The third major flaw associated with several spacepower theories is that they fail to address the consequences that the exercise of spacepower may have here on Earth, producing endorsements that prove to be farfetched or incredibly naive. Put in other words, these theories seem to consider space power as a fully independent and isolated actor, which can undisturbedly develop and deploy space assets and infrastructure and operate in space with barely no consequences. By doing so, these theories inevitably side-line the international setting—including internationally agreed upon principles, norms, rules and decision-making processes—in which a space power would be operating.

As actions in space have global impact, one country cannot decide to suddenly scale up spacepower capabilities that bear far-reaching military implications, without expecting any countermeasure. Single states and/or the whole international community will eventually feel threatened and consequently react to whoever credibly starts to build up such capabilities and/or start deploying assets in strategic positions/orbits. Thus, theories of spacepower that do not consider the international regime risk being not only farfetched, but also misleading. This risk, for instance, is well evident in Astropolitik, where Dolman calls on the U.S. to seize full control of LEO where "space-based laser or kinetic energy weapons could prevent any other state from deploying assets there", all without expecting retaliatory action as soon as this build-up of capabilities is noticed. In short, theories must at least acknowledge the existence of an international community of players and stakeholders, their responses, retaliations, sanctions, and consider that they will not simply observe the scaling up of threatening operations in space.

2.1.3.4 Space Power Status Neglected

The fourth major limitation is that current space power theories make empirical assessments and comparisons between different countries inherently difficult by making little attempt to provide reliable and usable criteria by which different countries can be compared.

This is due to the very conceptualisation of spacepower as a capacity rather than the actor having such capacity. Despite Lupton's efforts in 1988 to consistently define space power by underlining the twofold connotation of the concept, all subsequent definitions have tended to privilege only one connotation: i.e. they have explained the concept only in terms of capacity (spacepower) and not in terms of status (space power). As a result, today there is still no clear way to draw a line between space powers and "lesser" space actors, given that both can fit within a capacity-oriented definition.

On this point, it is worth recalling one of the most long-lived definitions of spacepower that has remained in use for 15 years -that adopted by the U.S. Joint Doctrine and the Department of Defence *Dictionary of Military and Associated Terms*, which defined spacepower as "the total strength of a nation's capabilities to conduct and influence activities to, in, through, and from space to achieve its objectives" (Joint Chiefs of Staff, 2002). What emerges from this kind of definition is that it implies that any nation with space-related capabilities should be considered a space power, although to varying degrees. The definition, in effect, neither helps to set thresholds differentiating between space powers and non-space powers (spacefaring actors, emerging space nations, or would-be space actors), nor provides precise elements to comparatively assess nations and actors.

With no common ground, no clarity and no prioritization about what fits (or fits best) the spectrum of spacepower capabilities and what does not, it is very hard to compare a nation's spacepower to others, as different nations have different space programme scopes and aims, as well as different degrees of technical and non-technical capabilities involved. Hence, how it is possible to make comparative assessments? How can different capabilities be compared?

A way to circumvent these flaws is to shift the analytical perspective by putting the spotlight on the status dimension of spacepower (i.e. the actor with spacepower) rather than on spacepower *tout court*. The status dimension is, in fact, broader, since it encompasses, but is not limited to, the capacity dimension of power. Importantly, this is not just a semantic exercise, as it opens up a new approach to both the development of a more consistent theoretical framework and to the comparative assessment of the worldwide space actors.

2.2 Space Power: A New Approach

Moving the focus of the analysis from a capacity-oriented approach (spacepower) to a status-oriented approach (space power) raises two tasks: first, to define a set of criteria that identifies space power status and differentiates it from other types of actors and, second, to empirically assess whether these criteria are met by the actors considered.

2.2.1 Space Power Constituents

In his *On the Edge of Earth—The Future of American Space Power*, Steven Lambakis was among the first authors to address the need for a status-oriented definition of space power, noting that today it is necessary not only to understand what or who is a full-fledged space power, but also to clearly distinguish it from a "simpler" spacefaring nation, given the potential confusion due to the myriad of emerging space actors.

Lambakis suggests that this distinction did not exist at first, as "in the past, a country generally qualified as a spacefaring nation, and by extension a space power, if it had a manned space program" (Lambakis, 2001, p. 45–46). Today, instead, given the increased number of actors—both public and private—with the capabilities and infrastructure to build, launch, or operate space assets (both in orbit and on the ground), it becomes indeed necessary to distinguish between spacefaring nations and space powers. Lambakis points at the ownership of an orbiting and functioning space asset as the indicator of being spacefaring. This considered, as more private actors have access to space and more spacecraft are operated and owned by them, the term "spacefaring" could also refer to various actors, not only nations.

As for a space power, Lambakis advises regarding it "as any entity that has the capacity to utilize effectively the space medium for commercial or national security purposes, with some pieces of its space operations coming from dedicated national satellites and other belonging to the private sector and/or government-initiated commercial activities". Lambakis goes on to briefly distinguish clever space powers and superior space powers: the first being those able to access, mix and exploit all the possibilities provided by space and space services; the second being those who "own and confidently apply significant space capabilities and possess, as part of their national infrastructure, the requisite skills to exploit them fully". Therefore, a hierarchy among space powers is established by the level of integration of space with national infrastructure and policies, with spacefaring actors remaining at the lowest level of the hierarchy as owners of space assets, without the need to structurally invest in spacepower capabilities.

Although it is an important step forward, for it does create criteria to differentiate space power status, this perspective is incomplete at best. By reducing space power status to the actors with the skills to effectively utilise the space medium, this approach overlooks the exceedingly relevant issue of autonomy (be it in the technological or in the political spheres). In fact, autonomy is a basic feature for explaining the concept of power as status: no powerhouse can be properly understood without considering the crucial aspect of whether it has the authority to autonomously make the laws and the ability to control outcomes (Cappelli, 2008).

Therefore, from a theoretical and analytical perspective, this study finds it more useful to regard a space power as an **entity with the means to autonomously deploy, operate and benefit from any space-related capability to support the achievement of national objectives**.

From this new characterisation, several important considerations emerge:

First, only nation-states can acquire and maintain the status of space power. While the definition theoretically opens the status to non-state actors, it is clear that only nation states have the means to master the full spectrum capabilities.

Second, whereas the definition of space power remains unvaried over time, its constituent elements evolve as a function of technological development. To illustrate, while in the 1950s and early 1960s, launching successfully was the primary feature characterizing space power status, by the mid-1960s, space power had materialized also through the conduct of major programmes in the field of human spaceflight. As space technology has matured over time and become increasingly sophisticated, the constituent elements of space power status have been extended to other relevant capacities, including regional or global navigation satellite systems (GNSS), telecommunications and Earth observation. In short, space power status is not a finite position but evolves as a function of technological development.

Third, this definition enables the determination of an intrinsic set of requirements setting the threshold separating space powers from other types of space nations. The definition, more specifically, highlights two crucial features defining space power status, here referred to as autonomy and capacity.

- Capacity is defined as the "state's ability to implement space strategies to achieve its economic, political, or social goals in society".
- Autonomy refers to the "state's ability to formulate space-related interests of its own, independent from or against the will of divergent political interests (either internal or external to the polity)".[1]

These two requirements will be further explained hereunder.

2.2.2 *Setting the Threshold(s)*

Drawing upon political science literature on the concept of "stateness" (Cappelli, 2008; Fukuyama, 2004; Linz & Stepan, 1996; Barkey & Parikh, 1991), we may elaborate that an effective space power exists if two sets of conditions are met.[2]

The first concerns the sphere of **capacity**:

- the state must possess a high level of capabilities in the full spectrum of activities; and
- it must be capable of effectively integrating space with national infrastructure, policies and strategies.

The second set of conditions regards the sphere of **autonomy**:

- the state must have the technical means to access and operate in space without the necessity of relying on any external source of supply; and
- the state must have the ability to formulate interests and define space policies of its own, independent from or against the will of divergent political interests, both internally and externally.

The extent to which these conditions are present in various countries is, of course, different and this difference determines the relative status and overall position of a given country in the space order. On the basis of these two sets of conditions, different

[1] Definitions taken from (Cappelli, 2008).

[2] The identification of this set of conditions and the subsequent construction of the space power matrix draw inspiration from an original theoretical framework developed by Italian political scientist Ottorino Cappelli and refined over the years in a few successive works, published both in Italian and English, including: "Democratizzazione o state-building? Riletture critiche della transizione", in O. Cappelli (ed.) Oltre la democratizzazione, Special issue of «Meridione», n. 3, 2005; "Pre-Modern State-Building in Post-Soviet Russia", in Ronald J. Hill and Ottorino Cappelli (eds.), Putin and Putinism, Routledge, London, 2010; "Lo Stato, la Storia, l'Antistato. Proposte per un percorso di ricerca interdisciplinare", Paper presented at the international Conference "Al di là del repubblicanesimo. Modernità politica e origini dello Stato", Napoli 16–17 April 2018.

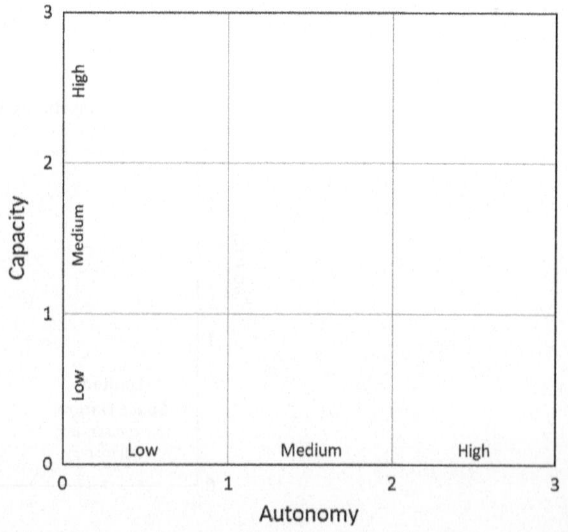

Fig. 2.1 Capacity and autonomy in matrix

configurations of status come into play. Some countries for instance, may score well on both the capacity and autonomy dimensions, while others may not meet any of the two sets of conditions. Between the two poles, there may be countries possessing only some attributes with respect to either the autonomy or capacity dimensions.

Given these variations, the question becomes how to exactly map and evaluate the position within the space arena.

A first answer can be offered by combining the two constituting dimensions of space power in a matrix (see Fig. 2.1). This presents a graphical representation of the political space determined by the relation between the level of capacity (axis y) and the level of autonomy (x).

The peculiar characteristic of this matrix is that it can be ideally divided by lines of demarcation that differentiate among a low, medium and high level of capacity and a low, medium and high level of autonomy, thus creating nine quadrants. In the upper-right quadrant, we find states endowed with a high level of capacity and autonomy that, consistent with the above provided definition, would fit the status of **Space Powers**. Conversely, on the bottom-left quadrant are states with a comparatively low level of capacity and autonomy, which can be ideally dubbed as **Limited Space Nations**. All other more nuanced situations resulting from a combination of low, medium and high capacity and autonomy were grouped into two ideal-types:

- A "**Spacefaring Nation**" is characterised by a capacity higher than the autonomy
- A "**Rising Space Nation**" is characterised by a capacity lower than the autonomy.

A graphical representation of these considerations is graphically captured by Fig. 2.2.

From an empirical point of view, it is possible to locate the various space nations in the matrix. For instance, at a first glance it would be possible to argue that a nation such as the U.S., which has been heavily investing with great results in the full-spectrum

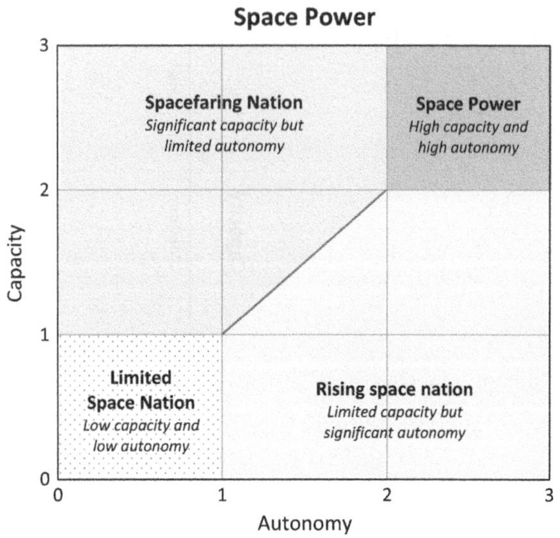

Fig. 2.2 Space actors in matrix

capabilities, would fall somewhere in the high capacity—high autonomy quadrant. Vice versa, a state such as Nigeria, which only recently has expressed interest in space activities and possess only few capabilities, would fall somewhere in the low capacity—low autonomy quadrant. However, differentiating among different levels of capacity or autonomy is not always a straightforward exercise. Therefore, in order to assess the exact location (and possible variation over time) of a given country, the two set of conditions must be defined and measured more precisely.

2.2.3 *Capacity and Autonomy in Matrix*

Capacity and autonomy can be measured in terms of scope and degree. Clearly, any country aiming to be a space power will need to have a high degree of capacity and autonomy in a wide scope of activities. The scope of these two dimensions is outlined hereby through two sets of indexes, each containing different indicators. In order to bring together different indicators, a score between 0 and 3 will be attributed. To take into account that the status of Space Power is relative (to other countries) rather than absolute, the score provides an evaluation of the indicator with respect to a qualitative/quantitative threshold usually based on the mean value for quantitative indicators and on the intermediate quality for qualitative indicators:

- 0: The indicator is null or not applicable
- 1: The indicator is significantly lower than the defined threshold
- 2: The indicator is neither significantly lower nor higher than the defined threshold
- 3: The indicator is significantly higher than the defined threshold.

To combine the indicators a 3-level Likert scale (Low/Medium/High) was used. The scale defines the positioning of the country/region with respect to the condition (set of capacity/autonomy indicators) and relatively to others:

- Low capacity/autonomy: indicators average below 1
- Medium capacity/autonomy: indicators average between 1 and 2
- High capacity/autonomy: indicators average above 2.

In order to evaluate the different indicators composing the two sets of indexes with this scoring system, both quantitative data sets and qualitative evaluations have been utilised. Quantitative evaluations have been primarily based on the data and statistics from the Space Activity Database of the European Space Policy Institute (ESPI). Qualitative evaluations are the result of the work of a dedicated focus group of six ESPI researchers, each possessing a geographical/sectorial expertise relevant to the conduct of the comparative assessment (see Annex A.3—Matrix Evaluation Elements for more details).

2.2.3.1 Capacity

The first set of criteria defining space power status relates to the sphere of capacity, which is generally defined as the state's ability to implement strategies to achieve its economic, political, or social goals in society. With specific respect to space, we may argue that effective capacity exists if a given state possesses a high level of capabilities in the full spectrum of activities, and is capable of effectively integrating space with the national infrastructure, policies and strategies.

In order to assess whether these conditions are met, a set of two *indexes* is deployed. The first relates to what can be termed as *hard capacity*, i.e. the material assets and abilities that allow an actor to operate in, through and from space in the full array of known space activities. Technical capacities are directly related to the spectrum of space activities. The second concerns what can be labelled as *soft capacity*, i.e. the capacity to effectively utilise and integrate assets and expertise in national policies, infrastructure and activities.

All the entries are eventually scored for each considered actor, thus obtaining a final evaluation of capacity.

Hard Capacity

With respect to hard capacity, the most important issue-areas to be considered and the relative parameters to be used when measuring capacity are summarised in Table 2.2. A more detailed description of the entries is provided in Annex A.3—Matrix Evaluation Elements.

Table 2.2 Areas of hard capacity

Areas	Entries
Access to space	Number of launches
	Launchers variety
	Performance
	Reliability
	Flexibility
Ground segment	Ground stations
	Launch facilities
	Integration and test facilities
	Mission control centres
Operational space systems	(Remote sensing) Number of satellites
	(Remote sensing) Variety of sensor types
	(Remote sensing) Variety of performance
	(Remote sensing) Mission diversity
	(Navigation) Performance
	(Navigation) Coverage
	(Navigation) Augmentation
	(Communications) Number of satellites
	(Communications) Technological prowess
	(Communications) Mission diversity
Science and exploration	Number of missions
	Space science
	Earth science
	Diversity of destination
	Spacecraft variety
	Number of operational missions
Human spaceflight	Astronauts
	Cargo capsules
	Crew capsules
	Infrastructure and modules
	EVAs
	Human-rated launcher
SSA and counter-space	Space surveillance and tracking

(continued)

Table 2.2 (continued)

Areas	Entries
	Space weather and NEOs
	Maturity of counter-space capabilities
	Variety of counter-space capabilities

Soft Capacity

With respect to soft capacity, it will be assessed whether space is effectively embedded in national infrastructure and leveraged to implement national policies in a variety of fields. Given the transversal nature of space activities, creating a comprehensive list of soft capacities can arguably be a Sisyphean task. In addition, in view of the specific—and often unique—purposes space assets play in a given national context, creating one such list may prove inherently cumbersome from a comparative perspective. Be this as it may, when looking at the historical utilisation of space assets worldwide, it is possible to distil a list of the most representative fields that shall be taken

Table 2.3 Areas of soft capacity

Areas	Entries
Socio-economic policies	Natural resources
	Energy production and distribution
	Meteorology and environment
	Infrastructure development
	Transport and mobility
	Rural and urban development
	Health, education and lifestyle
	Markets development
Foreign policy	Utilization of space for diplomatic purposes
	Creation of soft power narrative
	Active participation in international decision-making process
Security and defence	Integration of space in national security policies
	Use of space for surveillance, verification and risk assessment
	Use of space in crisis and disaster management
	Integration of space in national military strategy
	Use of space in military operations

into consideration to conduct a comparative assessment. Generally speaking, space activities can be said to support the fulfilment of the objectives set in three broad types of national policies, namely: socio-economic policies, foreign policy and security and defence. Within these three macro-areas, the most significant fields in which space assets find application are summarised in Table 2.3. A more detailed description of the entries is provided in Annex A.3—Matrix Evaluation Elements.

2.2.3.2 Capacity in Matrix

The values obtained from the evaluation of the two capacity indexes will be subsequently transposed into a sub-matrix that graphically combines a country's hard and soft capacities and presents its position in regard to other countries (Fig. 2.3). The heuristic utility of this exercise is fairly straightforward, as it enables a comprehensive overview of the capacity level of a selected actor.

Eventually, the values of the two capacity indexes will be aggregated in a total capacity value, as shown by the following equation. This total capacity value will be used to plot the capacity axis of the main matrix of space power.

$$Capacity = \sqrt{\frac{Hard\ Capacity^2 + Soft\ Capacity^2}{2}}$$

Fig. 2.3 The capacity sub-matrix

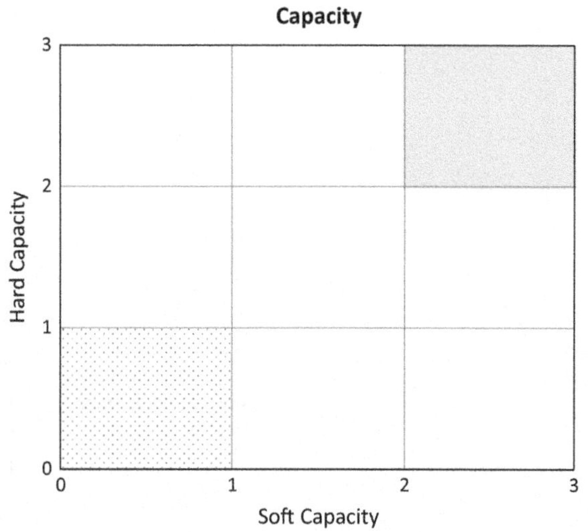

2.2.3.3 Autonomy

Autonomy—here intended as the state's independent ability to set directions, define policies and operate in the space realm by relying on its own strengths and resources—provides a second set of criteria to assess space power status.

As in the case of capacity, autonomy comprises two sub-dimensions: a technical and political one, i.e. it concerns not only the technological aspects of the space programme, but more broadly—and crucially—the political sphere, what political sciences literature would define as political sovereignty over space matters. Similar to capacity, all the entries hereby identified are consequently scored, thus obtaining a final evaluation for autonomy.

Technical Autonomy

Measuring technical autonomy requires assessing whether a state has the means to access and operate in space without the necessity of relying on any external source of supply. This does not necessarily imply autarky, for it may not be even desirable, but rather the possibility to ensure "mission independence" in case of necessity (e.g. trade disputes, natural disasters, or war). To measure this index, for each of the sectors considered under the capacity dimension, an evaluation will be made of what degree of autonomy (or critical dependency) exists with respect to:

- Production, and more specifically the underlying technologies required for the development and manufacturing of space assets, (including components, materials, processes);
- Operations;
- Exploitation.

The parameters that will be used in the empirical assessment are summarised in Table 2.4. A more detailed description of the entries is provided in Annex A.3—Matrix Evaluation Elements.

Table 2.4 Areas of technical autonomy

Areas	Entries
Production phase	Generic technologies
	Ground systems
	Launch systems
	Satellite systems
	Modules, capsules and probes
Operational phase	Launch
	Orbit operations
	Crewed activities
Exploitation phase	Data acquisition and management
	Service creation and provision

Political Autonomy

Political autonomy, as the second constitutive element of autonomy, is itself comprised of two broad dimensions related to sovereignty[3]:

- Domestic or internal sovereignty, which refers to the state's ability to formulate interests of its own, independent of or against the will of divergent political and societal interests. This dimension includes the state's independence in taking decisions without setbacks, slowdown, unclear and overlapping distribution of powers, responsibilities and competences, while favouring autonomous solutions over reliance on foreign ones.
- External sovereignty, which comprises the notions of international legal sovereignty, Westphalian sovereignty and interdependence sovereignty. In the space context, the word can be understood to refer to the state's ability to pursue national goals without relying on third parties and being influenced by possible invitations and interventions (coercions, impositions, etc.).

The major parameters to be considered when measuring the internal and external dimensions of political autonomy over space matters are summarised in Table 2.5. A more detailed description of the entries is provided in Annex A.3—Matrix Evaluation Elements.

Table 2.5 Areas of political autonomy

Areas	Entries
Internal sovereignty	De jure and de facto power to define interests and policies on its own
	Executive autonomy: ability to control outcomes of decision making
	Robustness to interferences from constituents and concurrent interests
	Preference for autonomous solutions
External sovereignty	Formal and actual decision-making based on the exclusion of external actors from authority structures within the polity
	Robustness to foreign invitations/political or diplomatic pressures
	Endurance to foreign restrictions/interventions

[3]As thoroughly analysed by S. Krasner, there are four different meanings of sovereignty: (1) International legal sovereignty, which "refers to the practices associated with mutual recognition, usually between territorial entities that have formal juridical independence."; (2) Westphalian sovereignty, which refers to political organization based on the exclusion of external actors from authority structures within a given territory"; (3) Domestic sovereignty, which "refers to the formal organization of political authority within the state and the ability of public authorities to exercise effective control within the borders of their own polity"; (4) interdependence sovereignty, which "refers to the ability of public authorities to regulate the flow of information, ideas, goods, people, pollutants, or capital across the borders of their state" (Krasner, 1999).

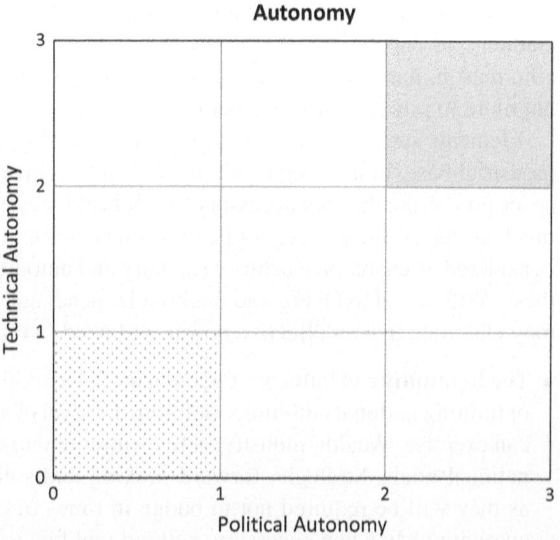

Fig. 2.4 The autonomy sub-matrix

2.2.3.4 Autonomy in Matrix

Similar to the approach presented for capacity, the scores of the two autonomy indexes will be visualized in Fig. 2.4, which combines an actor's technological and political autonomy and represents its relative position in the sphere of autonomy.

Eventually, the values of the two autonomy indexes will be aggregated in a total autonomy value, as shown in the equation. This total autonomy value will be used to plot the main matrix of space power.

$$Autonomy = \sqrt{\frac{Techical\ Autonomy^2 + Political\ Autonomy^2}{2}}$$

2.2.4 *Capacity and Autonomy: Underlying Requirements*

As mentioned earlier, the elements identified as part of the capacity and autonomy indexes are by no means exhaustive. It is therefore possible—and even necessary if new areas of space application emerge in the future—that other studies may integrate the previously presented indexes with other elements. For instance, in *Space Power Theory*, Oberg identified a list of "elements within a nation that make it capable of wielding space power", including some (e.g. economy, education, and industry) that have not been considered by the study (Oberg, Space Power Theory, 1999, pp. 44–47).

Nevertheless, it is important to highlight that some potential candidates as elements of capacity or autonomy have been intentionally disregarded for a specific reason, namely the fact that they are not solely related to space power status, but more to power status in general.

Elements such as an educated populace and skilled workforce, a state-of-the-art industrial base, or a strong economy, can indeed prove essential assets to become a space power, but they are necessary to reach and preserve the status of space power as much as that of air, sea, economic or military power. In this study, they are therefore considered as enablers to achieve capacity and autonomy, rather than components of these. With a nod to Oberg and the broader academic literature on great powers, we may elaborate that an effective power will need to rely on the following elements.

- The **Economy** can influence overall national activities for better or worse, enabling or limiting national ambitions, defining the level of autonomous action that a nation can exercise. Wealth, industry, active entrepreneurs and investors all contribute to national goals. Strategic, forward-looking and solid stakeholders are important, as they will be required not to budge in times of crises, or to carry on activities autonomously when necessary, without yielding to international pressure.
- **Demography** plays a crucial role in that size and age cohorts' impact on the economy, the workforce, and, relevantly enough, the number of taxpayers. A large population implies more funds, overall (human) resources, and hence flexibility to implement policies and strategies, and to pursue national endeavours.
- **Education** means informed policy and decision making, a highly skilled workforce, an informed citizenry, research and innovation to develop capabilities, and overall related spill-overs on the economy. Educated and informed citizens can more easily participate and react to national policies and overall policy-making, while understanding, coping and eventually supporting complex programmes and processes, be they public or private in nature.
- **Social identity and intellectual climate**, which can be made by traditions, shared values, mind-set and trends in social and national discourses. These shape politics, economics, and education, influencing national discussions and policy-making, creating interest and enthusiasm in specific topics, issues, and challenges. If a society is typically risk-adverse, this could reflect in lower entrepreneurial levels and hence economic vitality. Similarly, if a society is characterized by conservatism and lack of curiosity, it will be hard for politicians to propose or even conceive innovative solutions in their policies. Clearly, this point is very relevant for (would-be) powers, as they can leverage such traditions, values and climate to gather academic and political support to most effectively draft policies and strategies.
- **Natural resources**, which spans basic energy sources and food security to critical and/or rare materials. Strategic access, management and stocking of these are quite important, either through domestic production or via long-lasting allies and stable commercial paths, with availability often helped/hindered by geography.
- **Geography**, in fact, influences national development, tendentially favouring nations larger in size, as it allows them to draw from a larger amount of resources, waterways, harbours, and so on. Geography helps in exerting, or receiving,

influence on or from surrounding countries. Geography (and the climate coming from that) favours, stimulates or obstructs the building of national infrastructure, enabling or challenging specific activities and capabilities, as well as determining the level of autonomy with which these can be utilised.

- **Exclusivity of capabilities and knowledge**, defined by Oberg as "the most volatile aspect of power in general", implies powers being able to protect their unique capabilities while constantly developing new ones and not being caught up by competitors and rivals. This is influenced by—and influences—all the other enablers.
- **Effective institutions and diplomacy**, finally, enable powers in implementing the right policies, to do so efficiently without wasting resources, while neither appeasing nor provoking other powers and actors. Diplomacy enables nations to act without fearing counter reactions, with national policies potentially even supported by the international community.

These enablers play a critical role for space powers. The economy is certainly important, and equally relevant is the presence of forward-looking economic stakeholders, as space activities require long-term commitments, with the addition that interrupting a space programme will result in higher costs and efforts to restart it. A strong economy, with a great industrial base, allows for more capabilities, also enabling autonomy in wider contexts.

Similarly, population becomes relevant when considering publicly-funded space activities, which require the comprehension, approval, and support of taxpayers and their representatives. Here education comes into play, which provides an essential skilled and specialized workforce to develop better space capabilities, as well as allowing citizens to better grasp the implications and stakes of a space programme, while empowering policy-makers in delivering suitable space policies. Social identity and intellectual climate are also particularly important for space powers, as a nation is definitely more likely to support and understand space endeavours if there is a widespread social propensity toward curiosity, innovation, exploration and risk-tolerance, while the presence of traditions related to space can enable more widespread support for space initiatives, as citizens acknowledge such as part of their national identity. As for geography, access to the right latitudes and longitudes enables better launches and better deployment of tracking stations, with the presence of ideally eastward-oriented coastal or uninhabited areas being also relevant to safely launch. A spacefaring nation without such geographical features will be constrained, potentially dependent on third countries' infrastructures and permissions (or lack thereof).

Exclusivity of capabilities and knowledge enable space powers to be technically and operationally ahead of others, bringing specific benefits to citizens, and ideally being able to operate alone while at the same time being included in international discussions and endeavours thanks to unique and irreplaceable capabilities. Finally, effective governance and diplomacy are also vital for a would-be space power, as, for instance, a good diplomatic network can certainly help a nation in fostering its space activities internationally with other actors, while efficient budget allocation and budget management can streamline space-related decision making at home, hopefully reducing potential pretexts for anti-space advocates. Similarly, the right national policies and strategies can also be considered enablers: an innovation policy could definitely enable and improve space capabilities, incentives for risk capital investing could boost private investments in space, and so on.

Eventually, a question to ask is whether a single enabler can be more impactful than others. It is true that the decision to pursue space, economic, or any type of power status, and develop capacities and to do so autonomously—partially or along the full spectrum of potential capabilities, with a narrow or a wider scope, with a fair amount of independence, or totally relying on third countries' capabilities—is the result of political processes. Indeed, while listing the elements of spacepower, Oberg also pointed to the predominance of the political will, emerging from the intellectual climate, over any other (Oberg, 1999, p. 136). The intellectual climate and a nation's social identity, with the political will that can emerge from these, is therefore the most significant enabler. Political will can decide if a nation aspires to the status of power (and if so, what kind of power it should become), shaping national efforts to pursue specific capabilities, their scope, and the level of autonomy with which to do so.

2.3 The Stakes at Play: Space Power and National Interest

Having examined the various contributions to the spacepower studies and having introduced a new theoretical frame within which space actors can be compared and their spacepower measured, it is now useful to disentangle the underlying motives that push administrations in pursuing long-term, costly, and burdensome programmes in space, provided that they have the necessary means to do so.

In fact, the reasons for a nation to ensure autonomous capacities in the full spectrum of activities and aspire to reach the status of space power are multiple and generally associated with a set of strategic objectives that exceed the mere space dimension. A poignant illustration of this is the White Paper issued by the State Council Information Office of the People's Republic of China in December 2016. In the paragraph titled *Vision*, the Chinese government lists what it means for China to be "a space power in all respects":

> to make innovations independently, to make scientific discovery and research at the cutting edge, to promote strong and sustained economic and social development, to effectively and reliably guarantee national security, to exercise sound and efficient governance, and to carry out mutually beneficial international exchanges and cooperation; to have an advanced and open space science and technology industry, stable and reliable space infrastructure, pioneering and innovative professionals, and a rich and profound space spirit; to provide strong support for the realization of the Chinese Dream of the renewal of the Chinese nation, and make positive contributions to human civilization and progress (The State Council Information Office of the People's Republic of China, 2016).

Thus, reaching space power status has a large array of manifold, intertwined and not always straightforward implications, ranging from leadership, prestige and national pride to social and economic development, passing through a number of military and national security reasons.

While the primary focus may well differ among different actors, it can be argued that at the heart of states' pursuit of space power is the notion of national interest. The concept of national interest is used both in political and academic environments, and, just like the concept of power, it has been defined and explained through different approaches. Political science literature (George & Keohane, 1980) (Wendt, 1999, p. 235) has classified national interest into the three major categories of "physical security, economic well-being, political weight",[4] which equate to three broad types of stakes at play, namely:

- Security stakes
- Economic stakes
- Political stakes.

When applied to the concept of space power, this categorisation of stakes has been widely utilised within the literature, which generally considers space as an enabler for the pursuit of objectives associated with a country's national interest. Scott F. Swilley, for instance, has stressed that spacepower "is a significant contributor to military power", it "currently creates considerable economic power", and it "contains substantial demonstrated potential for political influence" both at home and abroad, adding that spacepower reinforces projection of power, as well as the means to foster one nation's overall status of power (Swilley, 2011, pp. 23–29).

Before providing further insights into these stakes, an important clarification should be made. Reaching the status of space power is not a prerequisite for deriving the benefits that stem from engagement in space. Obviously, there are benefits to be gained even when a nation does not reach the required level of capacity and autonomy to be considered a space power. Emerging space actors may in addition have the same security, economic, political, or status considerations in mind when deciding to pursue their own space programmes. Yet it is clear that only with the status of space power can interests associated with these stakes be pursued in the most effective fashion.[5] In other words, reaping the desired benefits to the maximum is reserved to those having the will and the capacity to invest the most. This notion should be kept in mind through the following part of the chapter, which deals with the

[4]Overall, the understanding of national interest usually sets this concept within the area of the most fundamental objectives that a state pursues within the international scene—to secure one's own existence, uphold freedom from threats from other actors and safeguard economic and social well-being of its constituents (in case of liberal democracies, society itself).

[5]A country launching an earth observation satellite can indeed benefit from it, but a lack of other upstream or downstream capacities might mean only partial exploitation of the satellite, ineffective management of the space asset, inefficient applications of its data, or poor integration. Similarly, developing capacities along the full spectrum of space activities, but doing so not independently, might mean being vulnerable to other nations' decisions and overall international externalities, as well as leaving industries inefficiently exploiting otherwise vital economies of scale, overall falling behind competitors (and suppliers). In short, there are benefits to be gained from simple involvement in space, but with clear drawbacks: missing the added value of having the full spectrum of capacities, and being able to decide to exert them with maximum autonomy when needed.

categorisation of space power stakes. Simultaneously, the understanding of a "stake" in this regard has to take into account the competitive international environment, in which a potential gain for one actor spells a loss for another.

The more ambitious the goals associated with pursuit of robust space programmes, the more relevant are the stakes resulting from a major presence in space. Today, this is reflected in increasing reliance on space technologies and services enabled through them in both security and economic policies and by other industry sectors. By scaling up this reasoning even higher, the more the country aspires to become a space power, the higher are the stakes at play in this undertaking. Both in terms of what the actor gets if it becomes a space power and what it potentially loses should it decide to not pursue such status. In such case, the link between space, more precisely the status of space power, and national interest, becomes more prominent.

2.3.1 Security Stakes

The endeavour to achieve and maintain space power status entails substantial security considerations, both in the traditional security domains encompassing space, military and defence, as well as in the broader understandings of the concept of security (crisis and disaster management, border monitoring and control, climate and weather forecasts).

Looking at the traditional security understandings, the stakes associated with space power status are visible in both the space and terrestrial mediums. Although considered a multi-dimensional concept, space power is distinctively magnified through the use of space systems in a military context. As force enablers, space systems enable empowerment of military strategies and the shaping of more ambitious and daunting objectives (Air Force Space Command, s.d.). This has been omnipresent ever since the first documented projections of spacepower in the early 1990s by the United States. For instance, in leveraging the use of signals from the GPS system, the U.S. military drastically improved the precision of its striking capabilities and the overall guiding of its troops overseas. The capabilities associated with space power have also allowed information dominance, which is a key element of power projection and the protection of territory and troops overseas through anti-ballistic missile defence capabilities (United States, 2002). Information dominance is largely enabled through the use of intelligence, surveillance, communication, and positioning, navigation and timing (PNT) satellites.

The utilization of space systems thus makes armed forces more resilient, helping them to act faster and decide better. Additionally, spacepower from the military angle usually supplements several capabilities relevant to improving decision-making, effectively contributing also to deterrence potential, though not as significantly as other strategic tools, such as possession of nuclear weapons. These tools include early warning, secured communications and surveillance and reconnaissance capabilities. Some other concepts, for instance space-based missile defence, have also been subject to research and political considerations, but not yet effectively deployed.

The discourse on spacepower has also touched upon considerations of the space domain as a medium through which warfare operations could eventually also be undertaken. Though space has not yet become this ultimate high-ground, a spectrum of fragments of such logic in national space policies or concrete activities of selected countries can still be found to support this claim at least partially. One such example is the pursuit of counterspace capabilities. Numerous publicly available resources underline both past and current R&D associated with counterspace; to a lesser extent one can also find indications of thinking on the utilization of space-based weapon systems to target terrestrial objects. Hence, the pursuit of spacepower, can fit in well in the build-up of power capabilities serving national security objectives.

The capabilities associated with space power have also allowed information dominance, which is a key element of power projection and the protection of territory and troops overseas. Information dominance is largely enabled through the use of intelligence, surveillance, communication, and PNT satellites. Thus, the pursuit of space power status brings about considerable contributions to the military domain, enhancing both defensive and offensive capabilities.

The contributions of space assets and services to the broader understandings of the concept of security need to be recognized in conjunction with the military domain. The enabling function of space is easily documented also in this rather civilian segment. It allows the actor to safeguard security and the well—being of its citizens through contributing to better climate and weather predictions, crisis management following natural and man-made disasters, monitoring of illegal movements on land and maritime border regions, and improved access to services needed in emergency situations. In this respect, space-based remote sensing, satellite communications or PNT services play an indispensable role in enhancing an actor's security, despite, in certain cases, not having any direct relation to military aspects of spacepower.

2.3.2 *Economic Stakes*

Alongside military stakes, mastering the full spectrum of capacities is associated with key economic stakes. The economic benefits associated with space activities are well known and documented in a number of studies and through a variety of approaches.

The key indicator, showcasing the economic value of space is the capacity of space investments to generate noteworthy return on investment (ROI), reaching comfortably the factor of 3 or 4. In 2014, the Organisation for Economic Cooperation and Development (OECD) mapped several national experiences in this regard, recognizing the ROI factors of public spending on space in OECD countries in the range of 1.5–5 (OECD, 2014). This means that each single euro invested in space resulted in a positive economic return—with generated incomes ultimately exceeding the initial costs. In a similar manner, the London Economics consultancy calculated the ROI factor of ESA programmes being generally in the range of 4–5 and in case of NASA programmes even higher, between 6 and 9 (London Economics, 2015). Again, PwC estimates that the benefits to be accrued between 2017 and 2035 from the Copernicus programme will be between 10 and 20 times the programme's cost (PwC, 2017a, b). Nevertheless, calculating the ROI in space programmes is not a straightforward exercise and the societal aspect of ROI comes to play. Given the transverse nature of space activities, the benefits of public spending on space contribute to the more effective execution of public policies or market development in industrial sectors essentially linked to services provided by space infrastructures.

Economic benefits underpinning the pursuit of space power status revolve around technology development, innovation potential, fostering of the growth of private industry and socio-economic benefits brought by space technologies. Possessing space power status ensures tapping into the economic benefits associated with space in the best possible manner. Spacepower can be pursued in the name of scientific, technological and industrial prowess and innovation; missions can be envisioned to inspire generations to come, ensuring the nation a highly skilled, curious, and motivated workforce, while keeping the national higher education apparatuses properly stimulated.

Some of the economic stakes associated with space power status could be considered as relatively newly arrived in comparison to national security, scientific or political rationales for spaceflight, relevant also (or in some cases mainly) in previous phases of the space era. The emergence and continuing growth of the commercial space sector, booming private investments on space and space-related activities and affordable access to space have shifted the present narrative in both typology of space actors and space activities today. Certainly, this does not mean that health of the private space sector in spacefaring country or space power directly adds up to the notion of spacepower. This rather opens up new ways of thinking, previously undealt with, that the economic considerations cannot be put aside when constituting the space power stakes. As noted above, whereas formerly, access to space could have been considered as the most likely the ultimate criterion for space power status, nowadays a spectrum of other capacities, conditions and/or specific technologies determine the quantification of space power status and thus need to be reflected when discussing economic stakes. Given the nature of the global space sector nowadays, fostering the pursuit of space power status naturally brings about benefits stimulating the growth of industry and deepening of links between the space sector and other industry sectors due to diverse applications and services enabled by space infrastructures and spin-off or spin-in potential, which are intrinsic to the space sector.

The potential of space to generate spin-offs and draw spin-ins is but one example demonstrating the impact of space on technology and innovation development. The continuously diversifying portfolio of space activities necessitates that the public sector needs to count on a well-established industrial base to achieve designated objectives. The space sector, in turn, provides the country with an increased capability in the development of new technologies, upkeep of innovation potential, and production of applications and services tremendously supporting other industrial sectors, be they transportation, agriculture, communications or others. Space also contributes to scientific knowledge and STEM education perspectives, which are both areas with potential to generate added value in a nation's economy.

Having in mind the social aspect of engagement in space, past and current experience in the international space sector demonstrate the added value of space in socio-economic considerations, contributing to mitigation of disasters aftermaths, equalizing regional differences and providing access to information, education, healthcare and telecommunications.

Altogether, the various economy-related motivations for pursuing space power status create an array of different benefits. It boosts the industrial base of an actor, augments its technologies, stimulates autonomous market development and eventually also generates applications and services responding to socio-economic issues and thus adding to general social and economic well-being.

2.3.3 Political Stakes

In contrast with the economic stakes, the political stakes associated with space power status have been omnipresent since the inception of the space age. For both established and aspiring space powers, achievements in this highly visible and prestigious technological arena have been responding to a variety of political objectives. A key driver is the enhancement of national prestige, utilised as a springboard for the realisation of broader political objectives in relation to both the domestic and the international arena.

Apart from being a highly visible demonstration of the technological prowess of a country, space endeavours, and human spaceflight in particular, are important "status markers" that put the country at the forefront in the international arena and contribute to its image as a major player. The overarching notion in this regard is that space power provides a country with important soft power tools, enhancing the exercise of political influence, in both domestic and foreign policies.

Domestically, successful space programmes can raise the reputation of a government in the eyes of its citizens, demonstrating a nation's capability to execute ambitious objectives with extremely high technological, financial or infrastructural requirements. Successful space endeavours contribute to national identity building and have the potential to serve as an inspirational drive for the population. As such, this effect can find its role not just in the domestic actions of executive or legislative branches but in political campaigning as well.

With respect to the impact of spacepower on the international environment, a space power is usually internationally acknowledged, creating in other nations mixed feelings of admiration, envy, respect, or threat. Producing a credible soft power narrative could be added as a potential application in this regard, one that can effectively utilize achievements in space and translate them into an enhanced exercise of political influence. This effect can materialize in bilateral relations as well as in multilateral setting. The soft power is also enhanced through international cooperation in the space domain, as it exemplifies the willingness of an actor to share the technological or financial burden and sacrifice individual gains in favour of mutual benefits. In some cases, space cooperation can even transcend broader international political tensions. The capability of space to attract international partners can also work the opposite way and stimulate negative reactions. When relations between countries are displaying adversity, distrust and suspiciousness, space can be a contributing factor to emotions such as fear, insecurity or vulnerability in the political environment of the opposing actor. Additionally, it should be noted that the impact of space on political influence does not need to be materialized in a specific interplay of countries. In this respect, spacepower fortifies the status of the actor in the broader international environment—it equips the actor with the ability to attract other not necessarily specified actors and thus augments its political influence in different regions of the world. From this angle, for instance, space could have been perceived as one of the contributing factors to the spread of U.S. popular culture throughout the latter part of the twentieth century.

Both home and abroad, as just evidenced, presence in space greatly adds to the perception of an actor, or in other words, to his reputation, recognition and self-esteem. Indeed, a final element to add to the pursuit of national interest through space is the category of status, which can be identified for aspiring and full-fledged space powers.[6] In the contemporary world order, space is one of the widely acknowledged status markers; spacepower reinforces the projection of power, as well as the means of fostering one nation's overall status of power (Swilley, 2011, pp. 23–29). Being a spacepower, in this reasoning, is essentially one of the denominators of great power status in world politics. That itself is a significant stake, encouraging actors in the international arena to consider aspiring for spacepower just for the sake of status (Paikowsky, 2010, p. 11).

References

Air Force Space Command. (n.d.). *Air Force Space Command: About Us: Heritage: 1980s–1990s*. Retrieved 12 13, 2018, from https://www.afspc.af.mil/About-Us/Heritage/1980s-1990s/.

Al-Rodhan, N. R. (2012). *Meta-geopolitics of outer space*. London: Palgrave Macmillan.

Barkey, K., & Parikh, S. (1991). Comparative perspective on the state. *International Review of Sociology, 17*(2), 523–549.

Barnett, M., & Duvall, R. (2005). Power in international politics. *International Organization, 59*(1), 39–75.

[6]To better elucidate this, it may be helpful to draw on the work of Deganit Paikowsky, who defines international politics surrounding the "Space Club", the elite group of nations which managed to rise above the others and become spacefaring (Paikowsky, 2010). The concept offers an interesting point of view: a club that, as for any club, provides benefits to its members, just for being part of it. Intuitively, this club mostly benefits those small and medium powers that manage to be part of it. "Declaring club membership is an attempt to place a state in a category of higher capability, power, and prestige at the expense of the strong and powerful", as lesser powers enclose themselves and Space Powers in the same exclusive group (Paikowsky, 2010, p. 11). Even full-fledged Space Powers, however, can become trapped in this club mind-set: once a nation reaches the status of Space Power, it is in its interest to maintain it, also emulating what other Powers and rivals are doing, just for the fear of missing out on trends or simply losing ground in front of the international community.

Blalock, H. M. (1989). *Power and conflict: Toward a general teory*. Newbury Park, CA: Sage.

Cappelli, O. (2008). Pre-modern state-building in post-Soviet Russia. *Journal of Communist Studies and Transition Politics*, *24*(4), 531–572.

Dahl, R. A. (1957). The concept of power. *Behavioral Science, 2*(3), 201–2015.

Dolman, E. C. (2001). *Astropolitik: Classical geopolitics in the space age*. London: Frank Cass Publishers.

London Economics. (2015). *Returns from public space investments*. London: London Economics.

Fox, J. G. (2001). Some principles on space strategy (or 'Corbett in Orbit'). *Space Policy, 17*(1), 7–11.

France, M. E. (2000). Back to the future: Space power theory and A. T. Mahan. *Space Policy, 16,* 237–241.

Fredriksson, B. E. (2006). *Globalness—Toward a space power theory*. Montgomery: Air University Press.

Fukuyama, F. (2004). *State-building: Governance and world order in the 21st century*. Ithaca: Cornell Univeristy Press.

George, A., & Keohane, R. (1980). The concept of national interests: uses and limitations. In A. George (Ed.), *Presidential decisionmaking in foreign policy* (pp. 217–238). Boulder: Westview Press.

Gray, C. S. (1996). The influence of space power upon history. *Comparative Strategy, 15*(4), 293–308.

Gray, C. S. (2001). Series Editor's Preface. In E. C. Dolman (Ed.), *Astropolitik: Classical geopolitics in the space age*. London: Frank Cass Publishers.

Harter, M. E. (2006). Ten propositions regarding space power: The dawn of a space force. *Air and Space Power Journal, 20*(2), 64–78.

Havercroft, J., & Duvall, R. (2009). Critical astropolitics: The geopolitics of space control and the transformation of state sovereignty. In N. Bormann & M. Sheehan (Eds.), *Securing outer space* (pp. 42–58). London: Routledge.

Hays, P. L. (2014). Spacepower Theory. In K.-U. Schrogl, P. L. Hays, J. Robinson, D. Moura, C. Giannopapa, K.-U. Schrogl, P. L. Hays, J. Robinson, D. Moura, & C. Giannopapa (Eds.), *Handbook of space security* (pp. 57–79). New York: Springer.

Hyatt, J. L., Paul, L. L., Rampino, M. A., Ricchi, R. R., & Schwarz, J. H. (1995). *Space power 2010*. Montgomery: Air University Press.

Johnson, D. J., Pace, S., & Gabbard, B. (1998). *Space: Emerging options for national power*. Santa Monica: RAND Corporation.

Joint Chiefs of Staff. (2002). *Joint doctrine for space operations*. Washington, DC: Joint Chiefs of Staff. Retrieved from Joint Chiefs of Staff.

Jusell, J. J. (1998). *Space power theory: a rising star*. Montgomery: Air University Press.

Klein, J. J. (2006). *Space warfare: Strategy, principles and policy*. Abingdon: Routledge.

Krasner, S. D. (1999). *Sovereignty: Organized hipocrisy*. Princeton, N.J.: Princeton University Press.

Lambakis, S. (2001). *On the edge of earth: The future of American space power*. Lexington: University Press of Kentucky.

Linz, J. J., & Stepan, A. (1996). *Problems of democratic transition and consolidation*. Baltimore: John Hopkins Univeristy Press.

Lupton, D. E. (1988). *On space warfare: A space power doctrine*. Montgomery: Air University Press.

Lutes, C. D. (2008). Spacepower in the 21st Century. *Joint Force Quarterly, 49,* 66–72.

Nye, J. S. (2003). *The paradox of American power: Why the world's only superpower can't go it alone*. Oxford: Oxford University Press.

Oberg, J. E. (1999). *Space power theory*. Colorado Springs: U.S. Air Force Academy.

Oberg, J. E. (2005). *Towards a theory of "space power"*. Retrieved December 13, 2018, from http://www.jamesoberg.com/space-power-theory.pdf.

OECD. (2014). *The space economy at a glace 2014*. Paris: OECD Publishing.

Paikowsky, D. (2010). *Membership in the space club: A tool in the hands of medium-sized and small states for empowerment and projection of power.*
PwC. (2017). *Copernicus ex-ante benefits assesment.* PwC.
PwC. (2017). *Dependence of the european economy on space infrastructures—Potential impacts of space assets loss.* European Union.
Swilley, S. F. (2011). *Space power: A theory for sustaining US security through the information age.* Leavenworth: School of Advanced Military Studies.
Tellis, A. J., Bially, J., Layne, C., McPherson, M., & Sollinger, J. M. (2000). *Measuring national power in the postindustrial age: Analyst's handbook.* RAND Corporation.
The State Council Information Office of the People's Republic of China. (2016). *China's space activities in 2016.* The State Council Information Office of the People's Republic of China. Retrieved from http://www.scio.gov.cn/zfbps/32832/Document/1537024/1537024.htm.
Air Force, U. S. (1998). *Air force doctrine document 2-2.* Montgomery: Air Force Doctrine Center.
United States. (2002). *The national security strategy of the United States of America.* Washington: President of the U.S.
Wagner, J. W. (2005). *Spacepower theory: Lessons from the masters.* Montgomery: Air University Press.
Wendt, A. (1999). *Social theory of international politics.* Cambridge: Cambridge University Press.

Chapter 3
Measuring Space Power: An Empirical Assessment

3.1 Introduction

This chapter provides an empirical assessment of space powers through the application of the theoretical framework devised in Chap. 2.2 Space Power: A New Approach. Even though the overarching aim of the study is to intensively investigate Europe's space power status (or lack thereof), it is important to put in perspective its relative position within the global space arena. The chapter analyses the most active space actors worldwide, those that instinctively can be collocated within or around the high capacity-high autonomy quadrant of the space power matrix, namely: Russia, U.S., China, Europe, Japan, and India.

Some preliminary data can be used to substantiate this selection and highlight the actors most visibly on the scene. These data include: the number of rocket launches, the number of spacecraft owned/operated, and the number of spacecraft manufactured per nation. In synthesis, what emerges from the comparison is that almost the totality of the launches is conducted by these six main actors—Russia, U.S., China, Europe, Japan, and India. Iran, Israel, and North Korea are the only other countries that have successfully launched a rocket in the last 18 years. The same six actors are the manufacturers and owners/operators of the huge majority of spacecraft launched worldwide. More countries are involved in manufacturing or operating spacecraft rather than launching them, with a seventh actor, Canada, standing out from these other nations.

Looking at Figs. 3.1 and 3.2, in the period from 2000 to 2017, a total of 1263 rockets were successfully launched, with more than 2500 spacecraft achieving orbit, and with the number of planned satellites suggesting that this amount will increase even more in the years to come. Despite the extent of these activities and a general trend showing increasing numbers of both private and public actors becoming involved with space, the great majority of launches and spacecraft still comes from the usual small group of nations: Russia, U.S., China, Europe, India, and Japan, with another handful of countries—namely Brazil, Iran, Israel, North Korea and

M. Aliberti et al., *Measuring Space Power*,
SpringerBriefs from the European Space Policy Institute,
https://doi.org/10.1007/978-3-030-15754-8_3

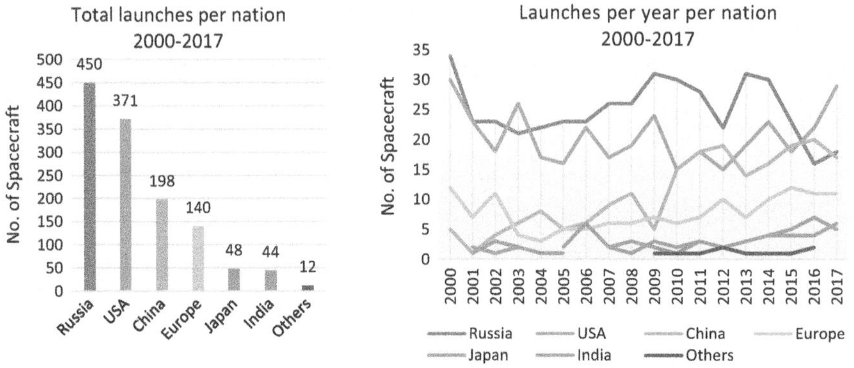

Fig. 3.1 Total number of launches and launches per year by nation, 2000–2017

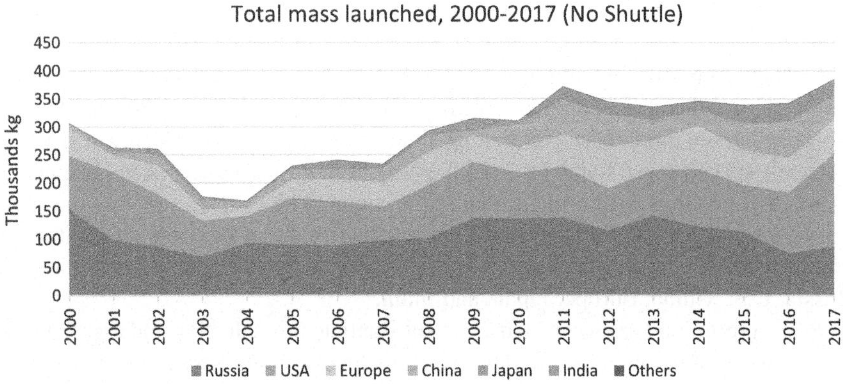

Fig. 3.2 Thousands of kgs launched by nation, 2000–2017

South Korea—making 20 attempts in 18 years, of which only 12 were successful, and only from Iran, Israel and North Korea. Looking at launches and total mass launched, the Cold War superpowers clearly distinguished themselves from the runners-up, with Russia leading the group both by number of launches and by mass launched, followed by the U.S.[1]

Analysing the spacecraft launched, the situation is not dissimilar. Presented in Fig. 3.3, data for satellites launched since 2000 show that more nations are involved in manufacturing and/or operating satellites of various sizes, with around 50 nations (considering Europe altogether) owning or operating at least one satellite, and around 30 countries manufacturing at least one. Nevertheless, the U.S., Russia, Europe, China, Japan and India are by far the most active, with the U.S. leading, followed by Russia and Europe. Relevantly, among the spacecraft launched since 2000 and not

[1]It is necessary to point out that the mass figure does not include the Space Shuttles, which would have offset the overall data.

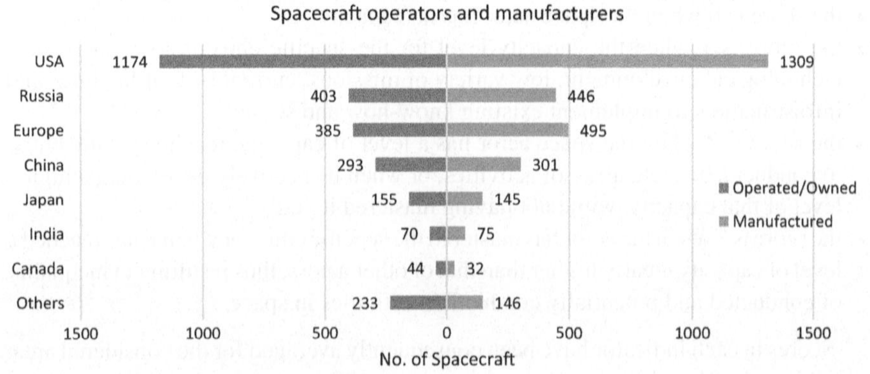

Fig. 3.3 Spacecraft manufactured and operated by nation

operated by the six main actors, 277 satellites are owned/operated by minor actors, with Canada emerging as the country with the highest number of satellites (44). Similarly, Canada stands out from the minor actors as the country with the highest number (32) of spacecraft manufactured. For comparison, Israel, which owns its own space launch capabilities, built 19 satellites and operated only 16 satellites among those orbited in the last 18 years.

Having confirmed that the six actors are indeed the leaders in worldwide space activities, the chapter now proceeds to analyse their capacity and autonomy.

3.2 Comparing Capacity

This section assesses the capabilities of the leading space actors using the elements listed in 2.2.3 Capacity and Autonomy in Matrix as part of the hard and soft capacity elements.

The data considered for the evaluation is related to activities conducted in the period 2000–2017, looking also at the spacecraft launched, the technology involved, the launchers, and so on, taking into consideration any type of spacecraft application—governmental, military or commercial. This specific timeframe has been chosen to better take into account the generally long gestation period for the deployment of space assets, but it has been preferred to a wider historical timeline to better capture the current state of affairs, which might not have emerged if looking at the historical data from 1957, although these could be relevant when evaluating the historical progression of space actors along the matrix.

The data gathered has been used to evaluate all entries making up the capacities (e.g.: the entry reliability, as part of access to space), for all the space actors considered, providing scores from 0 to 3. Whilst the criteria to assign the scores can vary from entry to entry, the rationale behind them is uniform:

- the score is 0 when the space actor has no capacity;
- the score is 1 when the capacity level for the specific entry is low, due to low technological development, low variety of missions, current lack of facilities and infrastructures to implement existing know-how and so on;
- the score is 2 when the space actor has a level of capacity, for the specific entry, to conduct a discrete array of activities, or when it is actively developing a higher level of that capacity, while not having mastered it yet;
- the score is 3 when the actor has mastered the specific entry, or when it has reached a level of capacity clearly higher than that of other actors, thus resulting in inequality of conducted and potentially conductible activities in space.

Scores in each indicator have been consequently averaged for the considered area, obtaining a single value per country for each area. The scores in identified areas have been ultimately averaged for one total score in hard capacity and one final score in soft capacity. Hard and soft capacities have thus been jointly plotted to form a matrix measuring the total capacity of these space actors.

3.2.1 Hard Capacity

As introduced in Chap. 2.2.3, the first index to measure capacity relates to the sphere of so-called hard capacities, i.e. the capacities required to build, own, and operate space assets and the infrastructures connected to them. Table 3.1 synthetises the scores for each country along the spectrum of identified hard capacities.

Unsurprisingly, the United States emerged from the evaluation with the highest score, with Russia being the second highest, albeit clearly lagging behind the U.S.

Access to space scores are higher for those with multiple different launchers. Besides the usual launch rate, performances and reliability, what really makes the difference is the flexibility of launchers in terms of compatibility with multiple payloads from manifold manufacturers. India scores the lowest, as few launchers and relatively lower reliability add up to performances to geostationary transfer orbit (GTO).

On the **Ground Segment** side, considering ground stations, facilities, major institutional mission control centres and launch facilities, the U.S. scores highest followed by Europe, with the other countries penalized mainly due to the lack of extensive ground stations and deep space networks.

The area **Operational Space Systems** comprises three sub-areas—remote sensing, navigation and communications. Remote sensing showcases American and European primacy in a sector that entails a variety of sensors, multiple programmes, missions and required performances of satellites. The U.S.'s number of satellites is very high, boosted by large constellations, as well as by the extensive use of remote sensing satellites for military purposes. China emerges as the country with the second largest fleet of remote sensing satellites, which is catching up to the American and European levels of technology. As for navigation, the U.S. and Europe score highest,

Table 3.1 Hard capacity scored

		CH	EU	IN	JP	RU	US
Access to space	Number of launches	2	2	1	1	3	3
	Number of launches	2	2	1	1	3	3
	Launchers variety	3	3	1	2	3	3
	Performance	3	3	1	2	2	3
	Reliability	3	3	2	2	2	3
	Flexibility	2	3	2	2	3	3
	Average	2.6	2.8	1.4	1.8	2.6	3
Ground segment	Ground stations	2	3	1	1	2	3
	Launch facilities	3	2	1	2	3	3
	Integration and test facilities	2	3	2	2	2	3
	Mission control centres	2	2	2	2	2	3
	Average	2.25	2.5	1.5	1.75	2.25	3
Operational space systems	(Remote sensing) Number of satellites	3	2	2	2	2	3
	(Remote Sensing) Variety of sensor types	2	3	1	2	2	3
	(Remote sensing) Variety of performance	2	3	1	2	2	3
	(Remote sensing) Mission diversity	3	3	2	2	3	3
	(Navigation) Performance	3	3	2	2	2	3
	(Navigation) Coverage	2	2	1	1	3	3
	(Navigation) Augmentation	1	3	2	2	1	3
	(Communications) Number of satellites	1	2	1	1	2	3
	(Communications) Technological prowess	1	3	1	2	1	3
	(Communications) Mission diversity	2	2	2	2	2	3
	Average	2	2.6	1.5	1.8	2	3
Science and exploration	Number of missions	1	2	1	1	1	3
	Space science	1	2	1	2	1	3
	Earth science	2	3	1	2	0	3
	Diversity of destination	1	3	1	2	1	3
	Spacecraft variety	2	2	1	2	1	3

(continued)

Table 3.1 (continued)

		CH	EU	IN	JP	RU	US
	Number of operational missions	1	1	1	1	0	3
	Average	1.33	2.17	1	1.67	0.67	3
Human spaceflight	Astronauts	3	3	0	2	3	3
	Cargo capsules	2	2	0	2	3	3
	Crew capsules	3	1	1	0	3	2
	Infrastructure and modules	3	2	1	2	3	3
	EVAs	1	1	0	1	3	3
	Human-rated launcher	3	0	1	0	3	2
	Average	2.5	1.5	0.5	1.17	3	2.67
SSA and counter-space	Space surveillance and tracking	2	1	1	1	2	3
	Space weather and NEOs	1	2	1	2	2	3
	Maturity of counter-space capabilities	3	1	2	1	3	3
	Variety of counter-space capabilities	3	1	1	1	3	3
	Average	2.25	1.25	1.25	1.25	2.5	3
Total score		2.11	2.16	1.18	1.57	2.09	2.95

particularly favoured by an already working and precise augmentation system, compared to those still to be fully implemented by Chinese and Russian counterparts. With this capacity, Japan and India are penalized due to the regional coverage of their respective systems, QZSS and NAVIC. On the telecommunications side, the U.S. and Europe again have the highest evaluation, largely due to the technological level of their satellites. The U.S. overall scores highest due to the total number of satellites owned and operated, as well as the overall major diversity of purpose of these, while Japan is prized, compared to others, by its technological progress.

The next area covers **science and exploration**. As for science, and in particular Earth and space science, the scores are low, with the U.S. being the sole country launching more than one mission per year, followed by Europe. Interestingly, Russia has few space science satellites, and none related to earth science. The data for space exploration reinforces the role of the U.S. as the leader in scientific missions, being the sole country to manage a discrete number of contemporary missions across the solar system, covering the quasi entirety of the spectrum of spacecraft types, be they probes, orbiters, landers, or rovers. To a lesser extent, Europe and Japan also have good evaluations, both prized for the exoticism of the destination reached, respectively the comet 67P/Churyumov-Gerasimenko and the two asteroids Itokawa and Ryugu. Russian scores are low, as the only space exploration mission attempted since 2000, although rather ambitious, failed to leave Earth's orbit.

Human spaceflight clearly favours actors with human-rated launch capabilities, with Russia's, U.S.'s and China's scores significantly ahead of others. Russia has the highest scores, as the U.S. has been impacted by the slow development of new human-rated launchers and capsules since the retirement of the Shuttle fleet. Europe and Japan manage to score due to their contributions to the ISS in terms of modules, infrastructures, and cargo resupply missions (here Japan scores higher than Europe, as the European Automated Transfer Vehicle (ATV) programme has been concluded, while Japanese HTVs still refuel the station). India, being last, might see its evaluation increase due to the announced intention to independently launch astronauts by 2022.

The final assessed area in hard capacity index, **SSA and counter-space**, relates to capabilities related most prominently in security and defence considerations. In the field of space situational awareness (SSA), U.S. and Russia lead in terms of space surveillance and tracking (SST), with the U.S. in general scoring higher than the other countries. Russia lags behind in particular in terms of initiatives to identify and track Near-Earth Objects (NEOs), although it is worth mentioning that all the actors do so in this regard, as the U.S. conducts the majority of the activities, followed by the Europeans, and by Japan, due to its minor contributions to sample-return missions from asteroids. Overall, there's much room for improvement in SSA. Finally, capacities for counter-space emerge as low or average among various actors, with Russia and the U.S. leading the group, but short of maximum scores. The low scores can be explained by the usual minimum institutional involvement by Europe and Japan in such issues, and, as for the U.S., Russia, China and **India**, due to the partial development of some of the capacities indicated, rather than fully across their spectrum. It is also true that the development of such counter-space measures is often controversial, constrained by international law, and a part of unclear, hidden programmes.

3.2.2 Soft Capacity

The second index to measure capacity relates to the sphere of soft capacity, i.e. the ability to integrate and utilise space assets in support of national strategies, policies, and economic sectors. Table 3.2 synthetises the scores for each country along the spectrum of identified soft capacities.

Once again, the U.S. has the overall highest scores, followed by China and Europe, then Russia, Japan, and lastly India. The runners-up alternatively manage to match the U.S. in specific areas of soft capacities: Europe and the U.S. received almost the same evaluation in the use and integration of space for socio-economic policies, while the U.S., China and Russia get the maximum scores in the application of space for security and defence purposes.

Going into details, as for **socio-economic policies**, the results highlight the wide integration of space within American activities, as well as European efforts to catch up by mean of the EU space programmes specifically developed to tackle

Table 3.2 Soft capacity scored

		CH	EU	IN	JP	RU	US
Utilisation of space for socio-economic policies	Natural resources	2	3	3	2	2	3
	Energy production and distribution	2	2	1	1	2	3
	Meteorology and environment	2	3	2	2	2	3
	Infrastructure development	2	3	1	2	2	3
	Transport and mobility	2	3	3	3	2	3
	Rural and urban development	2	2	2	2	1	2
	Health, education and lifestyle	2	3	2	2	2	3
	Market development	2	3	2	2	1	3
	Average	2	2.75	2	2	1.75	2.88
Utilisation of space for foreign policy	Utilization of space for diplomatic purposes	2	2	2	2	2	3
	Creation of soft power narrative	3	2	2	1	1	3
	Active participation in international decision-making process	3	3	1	2	3	3
	Average	2.67	2.33	1.67	1.67	2	3
Utilisation of space for security and defence	Integration of space in national security policies	3	2	1	2	3	3
	Use of space for surveillance, verification and risk assessment	3	2	2	2	3	3
	Use of space in crisis and disaster management	3	3	2	2	3	3
	Integration of space in national military strategy	3	1	2	2	3	3
	Use of space in military operations	3	2	1	2	3	3
	Average	3	2	1.6	2	3	3
Total score		2.56	2.36	1.76	1.89	2.25	2.96

socio-economic issues. The U.S. is favoured because of the overall wider adoption rate of satellite technologies across the economic spectrum, from agriculture to health, mobility, and lifestyle, with space-enabled applications and services being used more and more, also thanks to the surge in space-related activities and an overall market uptake. Together with Europe and Japan, the three are strongly prized by satellite-applications-related companies, including manufacturers of terminals and components, operating within their borders and making easier the adoption of satellite-enabled technologies for economic activities and policy making. China, more reliant on the public and military sectors, is witnessing major shifts within its space industries, signalling great potential for overall improvement led by stronger demand for space applications across the sectors, as well as by privatization and commercialization of the services. Russia, instead, shows a relatively lower level of integration of space in its socio-economic policies, reinforcing the idea of the Russian space programme as being mostly led by security and military considerations, with few real innovations and a lack of resources to fully implement and foster civil space capabilities. Finally, the assessment for India shows the progress made so far and the great expertise of the Indian Space Research Organisation (ISRO) in integrating space capabilities for socio-economic purposes, despite the overall level being lower than other space actors.

The U.S. is the clear predominant actor in using space for **foreign policy** matters, as Americans made of space a reason for prestige and international influence, a true soft power tool. The U.S. is the agenda-setting country in major international fora, and has captured the public imagination with its space activities, with both private and public American entities well acknowledged as the main actors in space. China, following the U.S., is the country that has invested more in space as a foreign policy tool in the last fifteen years, starting with the launch of a crewed capsule in 2003 seeking international prestige, bypassing U.S. restrictions on cooperation by enticing allies and other countries into buying Chinese satellites or rocket rides, while actively participating in diplomatic gatherings to promote Chinese space activities and cooperation, with its future Tiangong Space Station being a recent example. Europe comes third, with its efforts in promoting multilateral discussions on space matters, its free and open data policy for Copernicus and Galileo, and its active and quite relevant participation in international organizations such as the International Charter for Space and Major Disasters. Russia, on the other hand, has a comparatively lower score for foreign policy. Russian space endeavours are still coping with the aftermath of sanctions and struggling to maintain the pace of other international actors. Despite the U.S. and Europe being reliant on Russian components, launchers and spacecraft, Russia has only partially managed to turn this reliance into real diplomatic leverage. While India has just recently started raising its profile in the utilisation of space as a foreign policy tool, Japan has shown a higher and longer level of commitment in diplomatic and multilateral initiatives, with its active participation in the Asia-Pacific Regional Space Agency Forum (APRSAF) and the opening of its KIBO module for international educational purposes. Nevertheless, India has also its strengths, as it has managed to leverage its launchers to attract international customers and partners.

Finally, looking at **security and defence**, the U.S., Russia and China emerge as the actors with the highest scores, all three extensively using space for security and defence purposes, deploying space assets and integrating their applications both at strategic and tactical military levels, as well as for civil uses during times of crises and disasters. Russia and China have always dedicated particular attention to security and defence, investing heavily for this purpose, and stimulating discussions about whether the U.S. can hold its predominance in such realm, forcing the U.S. administration to envisage the deployment of a Space Force. Therefore, despite the differences in the available technologies and capabilities, the three countries have all managed to fully integrate space in this policy domain. Following them are Europe and Japan, both highly penalized by the political difficulty of discussing security and military issues: the political setting of Europe, via ESA and the EU, makes it hard to discuss joint security and military solutions, a setting which is also complicated by the involvement of NATO. Similarly, given the Japanese post-WWII anti-war constitution, Japanese governments have been restrained on these topics, forced to enact self-defence measures only, with only recent limited overtures towards re-discussing the issue, often conversing instead about sustainability as a softer version of security.

3.2.3 *A Matrix of Capacity*

Having assessed hard and soft capacities through their various elements, it is now possible to integrate and visualise the results (as reported in Table 3.3) in a capacity matrix that positions the considered actors on the basis of their overall capacity (Fig. 3.4).

The U.S. appears at the top-right corner of the matrix, being the highest-scoring both for soft and hard capacity. Indeed, the U.S. has the highest level of space capacities, covering the entirety of the spectrum of the activities, and doing so with a major level of technological predominance, and often exclusivity. Unsurprisingly, the U.S. clearly distances itself from the other actors.

Russia, Europe and China follow, with Russia being higher along the hard capacity axis, while Europe and China along the soft capacity one. Human spaceflight has a great—positive—weight on Russian capacities, while—as mentioned—the relatively neglected use of space for socio-economic reasons negatively impact Russian scores. More surprisingly, China and Europe find themselves almost in an identical position, and this is because the capacities in which Europe is stronger are balanced by those

Table 3.3 Hard and soft capacity by nation

	CH	EU	IN	JP	RU	US
Hard capacity	2.11	2.16	1.18	1.57	2.09	2.95
Soft capacity	2.56	2.36	1.76	1.89	2.25	2.96

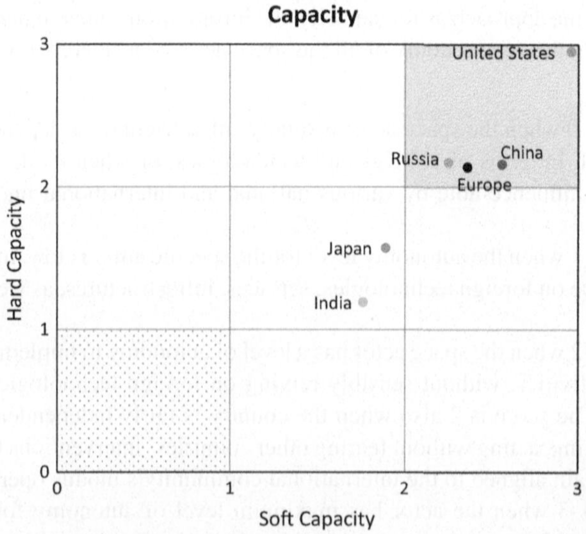

Fig. 3.4 Space actors mapped along capacity

on which it is less focused, such as military and security related matters. Both actors score almost identical in terms of soft capacity, while Russia falls short of exploiting and integrating space capabilities. Europe currently shows slight better capacities than those of China, but China's ongoing opening to commercialization and its fast-paced human space programme might mean a Chinese takeover of the European position, as well as that of Russia.

Japan, in particular compared to India, is prized for its higher level of technological development, its presence on the ISS, and its efforts in robotics and space exploration. Moreover, the country's newfound stronger posture on security issues, with the deployment of related space assets, contributes to its position on the matrix.

India shows a clear orientation toward soft capacity, a signature of its unique approach based on societal pull rather than technology push. The country might lack the technological and infrastructural depth of other actors, impacting on its overall hard capacities, but it still manages to score well as for "bringing space down to Earth", lagging behind Japan just in space applications for security-related policies.

3.3 Comparing Autonomy

Similar to capacity, autonomy is assessed by measuring the elements listed as technical and political autonomy. Compared to capacity, data for autonomy, and in particular for political autonomy, is much more qualitative in nature, resulting in the need for an overall wider qualitative assessment.

With the same approach as for capacity, the information gathered has been used to evaluate the shades of autonomy of all the space actors considered, providing scores from 0 to 3:

- the score is 0 when the space actor is totally subservient to or dependent on other nations both in terms of policies and technologies, or when its decision-makers are clearly influence-able by various national and international interests, and so on;
- the score is 1 when the autonomy level for the specific entry is low, indicating specific reliance on foreign technologies, services, infrastructures, as well as political decisions;
- the score is 2 when the space actor has a level of autonomy to implement a discrete array of activities, without sensibly relying on foreign technologies and infrastructures. The score is 2 also when the country is fairly independent in terms of policy-making, acting without fearing other countries' interventions but still being sure to remain aligned to the international community's modus operandi;
- the score is 3 when the actor has maximum level of autonomy for the specific entry, being able to conduct programmes and missions without the need to rely on third parties' technologies and infrastructures, but rather being the sole provider of certain services and facilities. Similarly, the score is 3 when the actor can act and implement policies irrespective of eventual counter measures, pressures or interest misalignments, being instead able to influence and shape the positions of others;
- the entry is ignored and it is assigned n/a, when there's a total lack of capacity (as with human spaceflight for India) which does not imply dependency.

Scores in each indicator have consequently averaged for each area, obtaining a single value per country for the considered area. The scores in identified areas have been ultimately averaged into one total score in technical autonomy and one final score in political autonomy. Technical and political autonomy are then plotted in the total autonomy matrix.

3.3.1 Technical Autonomy

Introduced in 2.2.3, the first criterion to evaluate the total autonomy of an actor is its technical autonomy. Divided along three generic phases of a space mission, the scores are reported in Table 3.4.

Overall scores show that China, India, United States and Russia have a high level of technical autonomy, followed by Japan and Europe. Interestingly, the relatively poorer performance by Europe and Japan can be related to their relationship with the U.S.: as allies, they have always benefited from better trade conditions, technology programmes, and joint space missions, lowering the need to develop indigenous capabilities.

Table 3.4 Technical autonomy scored

		CH	EU	IN	JP	RU	US
Production phase	Generic technologies	3	1	2	2	2	3
	Ground systems	3	2	2	2	2	3
	Launch systems	3	2	2	2	2	2
	Satellite systems	3	2	3	2	3	3
	Modules, capsules and probes	3	2	3	3	3	3
	Average	3	1.8	2.4	2.2	2.4	2.8
Operational phase	Launch	3	2	2	2	2	3
	Orbit operations	2	2	1	1	3	3
	Crewed activities	3	1	n/a	1	3	2
	Average	2.67	1.67	1	1.33	2.67	2.67
Exploitation phase	Data acquisition and management	2	2	2	2	2	3
	Service creation and provision	3	2	2	2	3	3
	Average	2.5	2	2	2	2.5	3
Total score		2.72	1.82	1.8	1.84	2.52	2.82

Looking into details, as for the **production phase**, what clearly emerges is Chinese total autonomy in this sense. Having been left out of major U.S. technology transfer programmes during the last fifty years, being highly penalized by the International Traffic in Arms Regulations (ITAR) regime, and being also excluded from the ISS, China was forced to develop everything domestically, eventually gaining almost complete autonomy. India, similarly, has been relying only lightly on foreign technology, priding itself on the domestic development of almost all of its space programme. The U.S.; despite its dominance in spacecraft production, still relies on Russian technologies (and in particular rocket engines), an issue pointed at multiple times by decision makers, and one which should be solved with the next generation of American launchers. Russia has been particularly hit by the fallout of the Ukrainian crisis, given the relevance of many Ukrainian suppliers to the Russian space programme (one above all, Yuzhnoye Design Bureau, the manufacturer of the Zenit rocket booster). Finally, the European economic-oriented approach to space has meant high reliance on foreign, cheaper technologies, from electrical, electronic and electromechanical (EEE) components to larger hardware, across all the production cycles of the various space-related assets.

Moving to the **operational phase**, China, Russia and the U.S. score highest, with the three having to rely slightly on others for at least one element each. In fact China, like all the other actors, relies to some extent on U.S. SSA information, while it has yet to develop a comprehensive network for deep-space missions, therefore relying on the European Space Tracking network (ESTRACK), for instance, for its *Chang'e* missions. Russia, more capable on the SSA side, sees its autonomy impacted by the fact that its busiest cosmodrome so far is not in Russia, but in Kazakhstan, and efforts to build a replacement within national borders are proving harder than expected. The U.S., instead, sees its autonomy limited in the field of human spaceflight, as it needs to rely on Russian carriers to launch crews into orbit, as well as on Russian training facilities to ready astronauts for this purpose. Japan and Europe score similarly, both relying heavily on foreign SSA information, as well as human spaceflight infrastructures and man-rated launchers. Finally, India still isn't fully independent as it has to rely on foreign launchers to orbit its heaviest payloads or, as mentioned, foreign data for orbit operations. India still has no capacities related to human spaceflight, so its score has not been considered in the overall result. Future Indian autonomy will therefore increase, or decrease, according to the extent of external support the country receives in the development of its human spaceflight capabilities.

Finally, on the **exploitation phase**, scores are more homogeneous, with the U.S. leading due to its wide array of space assets from which the country can extrapolate more and diversified data, hence not needing to rely on foreign satellites for space-based applications. Conversely, the other countries rely in some way on foreign assets, be they narrowband or broadband for (commercial) telecommunications, satellite imagery across the spectrum of various optical and radar based assets currently orbiting the planet, military-dedicated data, or the already mentioned SSA-related data. Similarly, for the creation and provision of services based on such data, the most autonomous countries are the U.S., China, Russia and India, with Europe and Japan relying more often on foreign suppliers and products, being more commercially driven.

3.3.2 Political Autonomy

Political autonomy, the fourth criterion to be analysed before plotting the final space power matrix, is the most relevant for Europe. In fact, and significantly enough, Table 3.5 shows that Europe scores the lowest, distanced significantly by the other actors. China emerges as the most autonomous politically, followed by Russia, with India and the U.S. third with the same level of high autonomy.

Concerning **internal sovereignty** and space matters, China and India have the highest level of autonomy, with effective distribution of power and competences, and streamlined decision-making processes that ease the implementation of decisions and the carrying on of space programmes. Russia follows, losing some ground just in terms of the influence of various national interests on the executives, often resulting in the lack of alignment to national goals by industries that try to push and pull the national space programmes. An attempt to marginalize this had been made with the creation of an umbrella state space corporation, but positive results are still unclear. Japan shows higher resilience from national diverging interests, but still lags behind for a yet to be clearly defined space policy, its post-WWII constitution, and

Table 3.5 Political autonomy scored

		CH	EU	IN	JP	RU	US
Internal sovereignty	De jure and de facto power to define interests and policies on its own	3	1	3	3	3	3
	Executive autonomy	3	1	3	2	3	2
	Robustness to interference from constituents and concurrent interests	3	1	3	3	2	2
	Preference for autonomous solutions	3	0	3	2	3	2
	Average	3	0.75	3	2.5	2.75	2.25
External sovereignty	Decision making autonomy from foreign interests	3	1	3	2	3	3
	Robustness to foreign invitations/political or diplomatic pressures	3	1	2	2	3	3
	Endurance to foreign restric-tions/interventions	2	2	2	2	2	3
	Average	2.67	1.67	2.33	2	2.67	3
Total score		2.84	1.21	2.67	2.25	2.71	2.63

branches of the government. The United States displays a great number of interests influencing the political process through the various constituencies where industries and space play a relevant role, while overall executive autonomy slightly suffers due to the dimensions of the executive and administrative apparatuses involved in space-related decision-making and activities. Europe, lastly, scores poorly due to its peculiar governmental status: an unclear and ineffective decision making process means also major influence-ability by the various stakeholders and interests involved, be they European-level institutions, European nations, trans-European and local industries, and so on, with a negligible preference for European solutions over foreign ones.

As for **external sovereignty**, the situation is not dissimilar. The U.S. scores the highest, being the most autonomous country, and less influence-able by potential sanctions or restrictions, and the one that more influences others and the international agenda also for space. Following the U.S., China and Russia score best. Both countries show maximum scores in terms of decision-making autonomy, as well as for resilience to foreign pressures. India finds itself constrained from pressures and self-limitations to avoid unintended provocations to, for instance, China or Pakistan, albeit still preserving a high level of autonomy from foreign interests. Finally, Japan and Europe score similarly to India, albeit being less autonomous in terms of international decision making, and having a slightly narrower freedom to act, and also being sensible to foreign pressures. The two actors, for instance, are often required to support their American ally, with an example being the American-led isolation of China in space activities.

3.3.3 A Matrix of Autonomy

As for capacity, the results from the two criteria used to evaluate technical and political autonomy have been reported in Table 3.6, and jointly plotted in Table 3.5, to represent the overall autonomy of the considered actors and to better compare them.

As shown in Matrix 6, China, United States and Russia are grouped in the first quadrant, being all endowed with a high level of technical and political autonomy. India and Japan display a high level of political autonomy and a medium level of technical autonomy, while Europe scores relatively lower compared to the other space actors in the two constituents dimension of autonomy (Figure 3.5).

Table 3.6 Technical and political autonomy by nation

	CH	EU	IN	JP	RU	US
Technical autonomy	2.72	1.82	1.8	1.84	2.52	2.82
Political autonomy	2.84	1.21	2.67	2.25	2.71	2.63

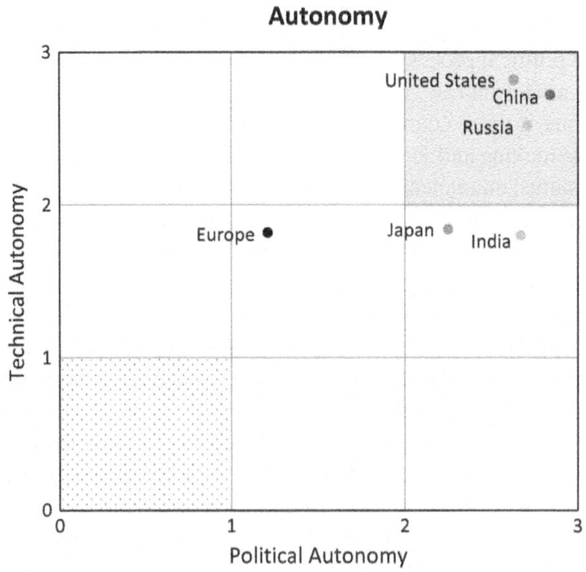

Fig. 3.5 Space actors mapped along autonomy

Sharing the same level of technical autonomy with the U.S., China's overall autonomy is among the highest. As discussed above, China's autonomy came and comes from forced isolation that has stimulated the development of indigenous technologies in an effort to match those of foreign actors, and from which China was barred. From this isolation, as well as its geopolitical aspirations, China has developed and earned also its political autonomy, currently relentlessly increasing the pace of its space activities, pragmatically considering or ignoring the various available international fora and the limitations that come with them.

Looking at political autonomy, the U.S. shows a certain struggle—at least compared to the majority of the other actors—in setting a national goal, navigating through the push and pulls of the various grouped interests and constituents, and the less-than-optimal streamlined execution and implementation processes for space policies. Nevertheless, when a national goal is set, the United States has the best tools and the strength to make such goals respected by foreign actors, not only being indifferent to foreign interests, but also influencing and driving others to align to its own. This position is reinforced by a high level of technical autonomy, which matches that of China and gives the U.S. the second highest score for total autonomy.

Russia and India show a similar level of autonomy, with the former being only more autonomous in terms of technologies. Russia, in fact, is favoured, compared to India, by higher autonomy related to space operations, having available more assets and experience. The country's position is negatively impacted, though, by dependencies in terms of hardware and components, scoring less than the U.S. and China. From a political viewpoint, both Russia and India have a higher level of autonomy related to domestic sovereignty than the U.S., Japan and Europe.

Achieving a fairly high level of autonomy, Japan still falls short of reaching the level of the already mentioned countries, penalized by relatively lower external sovereignty, as well as by the total reliance on foreign SSA assets and information, as well as human spaceflight-related facilities and launchers.

Europe, finally, comes last, both in terms of technical and political autonomy, being particularly penalized by its economic-oriented approach in space activities, its reliance on allies' assets and technologies, and a domestic transnational set of institutions, industries, decision-makers and overall stakeholders, which make it hard to identify and pursue a specific goal, and even harder when the goal is to achieve technical autonomy.

3.4 A Map of Space Powers

Synthesising the results so far in this chapter:

- the U.S., China, and Russia all have high capacity and high autonomy;
- Europe has one of the highest levels of capacity, but scores medium on autonomy;
- Japan and India, conversely, while lagging behind in terms of capacity, score higher in terms of autonomy.

Table 3.7 Total capacity and autonomy by nation

	CH	EU	IN	JP	RU	US
Hard capacity	2.11	2.16	1.18	1.57	2.09	2.95
Soft capacity	2.56	2.36	1.76	1.89	2.25	2.96
Technical autonomy	2.72	1.82	1.8	1.84	2.52	2.82
Political autonomy	2.84	1.21	2.67	2.25	2.71	2.63
Total capacity	2.35	2.26	1.5	1.74	2.17	2.96
Total autonomy	2.78	1.55	2.28	2.06	2.62	2.73

Once the various sub-criteria of capacity and autonomy have been analysed, we convert hard and soft capacity into a total capacity value, and technical and political autonomy in a total autonomy value, feeding the data from Tables 3.3 and 3.6 to the two equations:

$$Capacity = \sqrt{\frac{Hard\ Capacity^2 + Soft\ Capacity^2}{2}}$$

$$Autonomy = \sqrt{\frac{Techical\ Autonomy^2 + Political\ Autonomy^2}{2}}$$

The results are reported in Table 3.7.

Obtaining a final set of two values per actor, we plot the sets along the matrix of space power, locating the position for every actor (Fig. 3.6). The results show that the

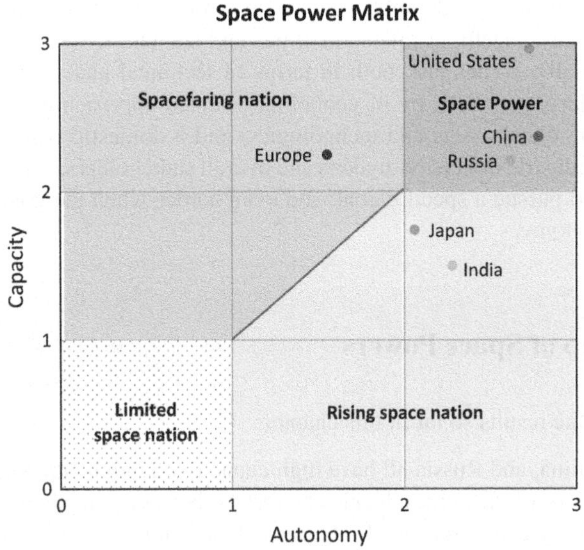

Fig. 3.6 Positioning major space actors in the matrix of space power

United States, China, Russia and Japan fall within the space powers quadrant, with Europe and India being respectively part of the spacefaring nations and the rising space nations quadrants, albeit with low margins.

The U.S. stands as the country closest to the ideal space power, with ideal meaning a country that scores 10 in both capacity and autonomy, therefore appearing at the top-right of the matrix. With a long tradition of space activities and without having had to face existential crises such as those overcome by Russia with the collapse of the USSR, the United States has had the opportunity to build up capacities across the whole spectrum of space activities, stabilize and master them, helping and helped by a high level of autonomy, which was on its side protected and sought after by sound policies, forward-looking decision makers, and an overall solidarity among national stakeholders, interests and industries.

It is significant that China appears to surpass Russia as the second global space power, both in terms of autonomy and capacity. Since the beginning of the twenty-first century, China has stepped up the pace of its launches, increased its launchers fleet, performance and reliability, constantly upgraded and polished its satellite technology, built an ever growing GNSS constellation, entered the human spaceflight domain, reached the Moon multiple times and, lastly, has been riding the wave of global private capital enthusiasm for space activities. China has been doing this in quasi total autonomy, forced to develop in-house substitute technology, barred from exploiting the global demand for satellite launches, and isolated in terms of cooperation in space.

Conversely, Russia's position in the matrix is the result of a space programme and an industry that was once prolific and now struggles to keep pace with foreign actors, slowed down by stumbles such as satellites and probe failures, the (also literal) downward spiral of the Proton booster, the abandonment of the Ukrainian-built Zenit for political reasons, and the rising costs and timeframe of building a substitute for the Baikonur Cosmodrome as well as the replacements for the half century old spacecraft and carrier Soyuz. Russia still manages to show its influence and capabilities in space, but its space ecosystem is starting to appear ridden by inefficiencies, corruption, discontent and fatigue, with a relevant level of technological and financial dependence on foreign actors. The country will face many challenges as the requirements for being considered a space power keep changing, progressing and shifting towards more complex technologies, more encompassing policies, and a larger societal involvement.

Slightly outside the space powers quadrant, Japan has been making its niche among the most active space actors, reinventing its space administration while pursuing incredibly challenging endeavours. Despite having been around for only 15 years, the Japan Aerospace Exploration Agency (JAXA) can pride itself with two sample return missions from an asteroid, a lunar probe, a Venus lander, a space station module, cargo capsules, astronauts, and more. More generally, Japan presents a strong, technologically advanced industry aligned and in pace with national goals, a thriving university environment working on space, and a political class that takes space seriously enough to link space policy decisions directly to the cabinet office, the agency in charge of implementing the Japanese's government policies.

Similar to Japan, India stands as a rising space nation. In fact, India has managed to develop its capacities autonomously, with the same autonomy level of Russia, even more than Japan, albeit not mastering the capacities themselves, therefore remaining below the capacity threshold to be considered a space power. As mentioned, the Indian approach has been generally associated with the utilitarian use of space to provide services and assistance to implement nation-wide socio-economic policies. This implies the will to build domestic satellites to help spread education and develop in-house technology, rather than seeking the cheapest solutions. So far, India has not pursued space activities for the sake of the status that follows, but rather to tackle real issues with what would have solved them better, meaning space applications in this sense. Things are progressively changing, though: with more high-profile missions related to space exploration and human space programme as well as a more active involvement in security and defence activities (as *inter alia* evidenced by the 2019 ASAT test) India could quickly gain enough additional capabilities and prestige to complete its rise, moving from the rising space nations to the space powers quadrant.

Symmetrically opposed to India is Europe. Europe has proven itself as the actor with one of the highest levels of combined hard and soft capacity, even more than China, with its greatly developed telecom and earth observation satellite industry, the finally operational Galileo constellation, the Copernicus programme, the numerous start-ups sprouting across the continent, and ambitious scientific and exploration missions such as Rosetta and the recently launched BepiColombo. Europe has also managed to integrate space in its overall policies, with the European Commission deeply involved in cultivating the European space ecosystem.

Yet, Europe still lags behind in terms of autonomy, and in particular political autonomy, to be able to quickly, effectively and straightforwardly take decisions related to space activities. European space industries struggle to compete with foreign companies and are less willing to take risks, waiting instead for institutional stakeholder to lead decisions that require long time and effort to be reached due to the tangle of relations, institutions, member states, and overlapping competences. For this reasons Europe remains more of a spacefaring actor than a space power, missing particularly what has here been called internal sovereignty. As stated in 2.2.1 Space Power Constituents, only nation-states can acquire and maintain the status of space power: the lack of internal sovereignty clearly makes it very hard for Europe to be compared to one. A dedicated reflection on Europe's extant status is provided in the next chapter.

Chapter 4
Reflections on Europe

Building on the outcome of comparative assessment of the major space actors presented in Chap. 3, this chapter will provide more specific considerations to examine Europe's position within the space arena and to put in perspective its strategic ambitions with the necessary means and resources required to meet Europe's goals.

More specifically, the chapter will first try to characterise what particular kind of actor Europe is, by further explaining the scores of the matrix and clarifying why it cannot be considered a full-fledged space power. Building on this, it will discuss whether Europe *should* ambition to become one, by disentangling the economic, political and security stakes at play. Finally, the chapter will elaborate on whether Europe *can* become a space power, by identifying the means and conditions to fulfil this goal.

4.1 Europe: A Space Power in the Making or Losing Ground?

As has emerged from the data used to plot the various matrixes, Europe possesses a high level of capacity, both hard and soft, but a relatively lower level of autonomy as compared to other major space actors. The two dimensions are further explained hereunder.

4.1.1 A Highly Capable Actor…

4.1.1.1 Hard Capacities

Having conducted space activities since the 1960s, Europe is one of the most experienced actors in the international arena and operates a highly regarded space

M. Aliberti et al., *Measuring Space Power*,
SpringerBriefs from the European Space Policy Institute,
https://doi.org/10.1007/978-3-030-15754-8_4

programme. Through its different constituents (member states, pan-European institutions, private sector), and as highlighted in Chap. 3, Europe has mastered, mostly through ESA, a wide array of capabilities that address the whole range of space activities, including access to space, telecommunications and operational Earth observation, space sciences, and navigation and human spaceflight.

Starting from the area of space transportation, Europe can boast an independent access-to-space capability that comprises all the required industrial setup, an operational spaceport, and a fleet of three operational launch vehicles (Ariane, Vega and the Europeanised Soyuz-ST). For almost four decades, the Ariane launcher has been serving a variety of institutional and commercial missions, becoming a symbol of Europe's achievements in space. The five different generations that have succeeded one another in the Ariane family have won a considerable share of the global market, launching half of the world's open commercial satellites and enabling Europe to construct a robust satellite launch industry and infrastructure.

Thanks to the subsequent introduction of the medium-lift Soyuz launcher and the lightweight Vega, the European family of launchers has expanded to ensure performance and flexibility, with the payload segment covered by the three different launcher categories allowing the entire range of launch requirements to be addressed. Today Europe can count on one of the most reliable and versatile family of launchers worldwide. They perform an average of 7–8 launches per year covering small, medium and heavy lift capacities with a discrete payload capacity to LEO and GTO. Besides their flexibility and reliability, European launchers exploit a great compatibility with payload manufacturing standards, also thanks the great role played by European satellite manufacturers on the worldwide market. Notably, European industry is also finalising the development of a new generation of launch vehicles (Ariane 6 and Vega-C) that will be flexible and modular enough for responding to the changing requirements foreseen over the next decade.

Besides its well-known launch vehicles, Europe owns a domestic spaceport advantageously located near the equator in French Guyana, and several European countries are currently discussing the potential development of other spaceports in different latitudes, such as the Azores islands, Scotland and Norway. Finally, the European ground segment is well developed, spanning worldwide and encompassing national facilities, the ESTRACK, and a highly diffused commercial teleports network.

In the field of satellite systems and applications, European public and private actors operate/own a wide space infrastructure comprising more than 350 spacecraft (Fig. 4.1) and related ground segments.

Interestingly, the majority of these spacecraft is operated by private entities, such as the SES Group and Eutelsat. This is a direct result of the prominent position occupied by European satellite operators on global markets, in particular for satellite telecommunications. European manufacturers are, as mentioned, highly regarded for their industrial capabilities, and the European institutions are actively involved in stimulating and procuring innovative satellite designs, as well as developing critical technology. Meteorology, Earth observation, telecommunications and navigation (Galileo/EGNOS) are the spearhead of the European space programme, with prominent examples such as the recent Aeolus satellite of ESA's Living Planet Programme

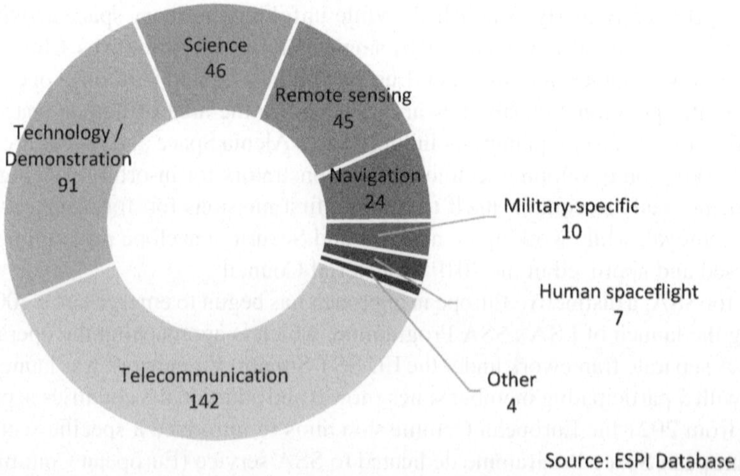

Fig. 4.1 Spacecraft launched in the period 2000–2017 and operated/owned by European actors

and the ESA-built Sentinels within the Copernicus programme. In terms of telecommunication satellites, the ESA Advanced Research in Telecommunications Systems (ARTES) has just reached its 25th year, celebrating a long period of joint research in the most advanced solutions for comsats, as all-electric satellites, small GEO buses, or reconfigurable communication satellites. As for navigation and positioning, the Galileo constellation, which is almost fully operational, already provides great precision services, and its interoperability with other systems is acknowledged as essential worldwide, providing "significant public interest benefits" (Federal Communications Commission, 2018).

Moreover, Europe is an established player in science and exploration, boasting long-term experience and invaluable contributions to science, robotics missions and human spaceflight. Over the years, it has maintained the edge of the state-of-the-art technological level and acquired a solid set of critical capabilities, often making it a so-called "partner of choice" for international cooperation. In addition to groundbreaking missions such as Rosetta, and scientifically invaluable projects like Gaia and LISA, Europe has also demonstrated the ability to provide essential elements to large robotic missions (e.g. Cassini-Huygens) and to the ISS infrastructure (e.g. the Columbus Orbital laboratory, the ATVs, and other infrastructure elements such as the Multi-Purpose Logistics Modules (MPLM)). Recent and ongoing European missions to the solar system, such as BepiColombo, are additional evidence of Europe's high-capacity and commitment to the field of space exploration and are all building an excellent "heritage" for future robotic and human missions.

On a less positive note, Europe lacks some capacity in the increasingly important fields of SSA and space defence. In the latter domain, European stakeholders do not display the degree of political interest in development and deployment of counter-space capabilities comparable to other recognized space powers. This in part stems from the European stance vis-à-vis the need to ensure responsible behaviour in space and, in part, from the fact that the military dimension of European space activities has not yet been properly established. While unfolding, military space activities in Europe remain limited and mostly led by single member state initiatives. Closely connected to this, another field in which Europe still lags behind is in-orbit operations. At present, operational capabilities are relegated to the area of human spaceflight activities. European companies, including Thales Alenia Space and Airbus are, however, working on developing technology demonstrators for in-orbit servicing, with ESA being ready to commit itself to funding first missions for, for instance, active debris removal, while working on a Safety and Security envelope programme to be discussed and approved in the 2019 Ministerial Council.

As for SSA, a distinctive European approach has begun to emerge since 2008 following the launch of ESA's SSA Programme, which is approaching the operational stage. A separate framework under the EU SST Support Framework was launched in 2014 with 5 participating member states (now 8 and additional 8 countries aspiring). Also, from 2021 the European Commission aims to introduce a specific section of the European Space Programme dedicated to SSA service (European Commission, 2018b). In addition, military aspects of transnational SSA cooperation were recently covered in the second round of projects selected within the PESCO framework. In this case, France and Italy have been leading the efforts. Despite these multiple initiatives, the actual level of European capabilities is by no means comparable to that of the United States. This is also evidenced by the fact that the EU SST portal (established for actual services provision), generates conjunction data messages (CDMs) for EU SST users using mostly data uploaded through data sharing agreements, predominantly from U.S. sensors—78% of GEO CDMs and 97% of LEO CDMs are generated through sensors outside of the EU SST Support Framework (European Commission, 2018c). Limited political will for a substantial increase in funding, deeper integration, and the establishment of civil frameworks counting on usually nationally (and military) owned SSA sensors are the main reasons why Europe lacks capacity in this domain. As such, although the enhancement of European SSA capabilities has somewhat begun and is progressing on national levels as well as through European initiatives, Europe still relies heavily on the capabilities of its partners, mostly the United States.

Overall, despite these missing capacities—for which activities and efforts are under development or undergoing—the European level of capacity is significant and matches that of other prominent space actors.

4.1.1.2 Soft Capacities: Integrating Space Assets in Europe's Policies

In addition to its hard capacities, equally striking is Europe's ability to integrate space with its policy objectives, particularly socio-economic ones. From this perspective, European space programmes have been highly successful, with the space infrastructure now enabling and enhancing a plethora of economic activities and with European citizens utilising space-based services in many aspects of their everyday lives.

Socio-economic Policies

The value of European space assets lies first and foremost in the substantial socio-economic benefits they enable across a multitude of economic and strategic sectors for Europe. This is not surprising, as European space activities have been traditionally oriented toward harnessing socio-economic benefits, justifying expenditure in space with its cascading positive effects on the overall economy. ESA's industrial policy and its mandatory geo-returns have always represented this well, but this is also the case for the more recent EU-led efforts in space, namely Copernicus and Galileo, as the two programmes have been specifically envisioned to support the EU's socio-economic policies. In fact, the linchpin of the European Union's space programme is the DG GROW—a reminder that European activities in space, and in particular those developed at the communitarian level, are and will be significantly driven by the political willingness to fully exploit the socio-economic value of the European space infrastructure.

European space infrastructure brings noticeable benefits to European society at large and is critical to the fulfilment of a variety of European Union and member state governmental objectives. Indeed, space assets have become instrumental for the implementation of key European policies, in both direct and indirect ways.[1] Examples of these contributions include, among others, the Common Agricultural Policy (CAP) to foster agricultural productivity, viable food production, reduction of agriculture environmental footprint and farmers' access to ICT; the Common Fisheries Policy (CFP) to support the sustainable exploitation of fisheries resources; the EU Road Safety framework to enable competitive, sustainable, secure and safe transport services; the EU Digital Agenda to bridge the digital divide in Europe; the Energy Union to give consumers secure, sustainable, competitive, and affordable energy (PwC, 2016); and the various environment-related policies.[2] Additionally, the uptake of space technology plays a huge part in Innovation Policy, laying the foundations for the cross-pollinisation of space technologies with ground technologies, and the development of new services in which space systems are key enablers (e.g. 5G networks, precision agriculture, forestry, air traffic management, smart energy grids, and autonomous vehicles) (Aliberti, Sarret, Hrozensky, Perrichon, & Rowley, 2018).

In short, space assets are today used in the vast majority of European policy areas and support in multiple ways the European effort to tackle modern societal and environmental challenges. The magnitude of benefits they enable varies between policy areas but can be critical when space assets provide a particularly efficient, and sometimes irreplaceable, means to achieving policy objectives.

---

[1]Space infrastructure can either contribute directly to the implementation of policies (i.e. space-based solutions are used directly by the EU to achieve flagship objectives), or indirectly (i.e. space-based solutions are used by actors of target sectors to improve productivity or reduce the environmental footprint, for example, which supports the achievement of EU objectives).

[2]Notably, in an historical juncture when other countries and actors are backing off from environmental science and studies, Europe has emerged as a leading actor in meteorology and environment monitoring, providing access to vital data worldwide.

Table 4.1 Adoption rate of space-based solutions in the European economic sectors

European economic sectors	Adoption rate (% of GVA)	Dependent GVA (EUR billion)
Agriculture	25.5	42.0
Forestry and logging	70.0	18.3
Fishing	41.3	2.6
Mining and quarrying	80.0	69.6
Energy	8.2	19.0
Construction	27.1	173.5
Land transport	54	172.5
Air transport	75.0	33.2
Water transport	71.5	25.9
Information and communication	13.3	67.8
Finance and insurance	24.5	167.6
Total sectors	28.6	792.0

Source PwC (2017)

That the space infrastructure is today well integrated in the European economy becomes even more evident when looking at the adoption rate of space-based applications and the amount of dependent Gross Value Added on these applications (Table 4.1).

As emerges from the table, there is a severe economic dependency on space assets in the majority of European economic sectors, and a particularly critical one in sectors such as agriculture and finance, with potential disruptive effects in case of space assets loss, not only in economic terms, but also social and environmental (PwC, 2017).

This reliance on space is the consequence of Europe's efforts to fully exploit space applications within its various economic sectors. The exploitation of space services stimulates growth and provides Europe with considerable benefits at the macro-economic level. Financial assessments of the downstream sector and economic benefits to end-user sectors assess that more than 10% of the EU GDP is linked to the space infrastructure and that the total economic benefit is around € 53.5 billion per year in Gross Value Added, supporting 1 million workers directly or indirectly (PwC, 2016).

The importance of space for Europe's economy is also evidenced by the value of its space sector. In 2017, total sales for the sector were EUR 8.76 billion, a +6.2% growth topping a seven-year long trend, stimulated both by institutions (59% of the sales) and other commercial actors (41%) (Eurospace, 2018). In the same year, European launchers orbited 24% of the global commercial satellites, with commercial launches revenues of approx. EUR 911 million (Bordacchini & Burger, 2018). Moreover, 58 out of 289 commercial satellites launched in 2017 were built by European contractors, representing the majority (53%) of total commercial satellites weight orbited in 2017 (ESPI Database), and providing a positive result for European satellite manufacturers.

Along its traditional "primes", Europe can also boast a thriving entrepreneurial space ecosystem, encompassing an increasing number of start-ups, dedicated incubators—i.e. the ESA Business Incubation Centres (BICs)—as well as business angels and venture capitalists' networks that are increasingly interested in space. This undeniable success is the result of the multiple efforts carried out by European institutions (mostly the EU and ESA) to create larger entrepreneurial and customer bases, widen the European space downstream market, and eventually boost further the European economy's linkages with space.[3] Incidentally, the next European Multiannual Financial Framework (MFF) will be prepared along the line of a transition toward the exploitation phase of Copernicus and Galileo/EGNOS—exploitation that will be based on a service-driven policy (European Space Policy Institute, 2018). This signifies an even greater commitment to integrating space with socio-economic policies for Europe, and an indicator of its high soft capacity.

Foreign Policy

Open data, high visibility in international fora, ground-breaking programmes and a wide network of cooperative relations are part of Europe's tools to support its foreign policy objectives. International cooperation has traditionally been one of the most striking features of Europe' s space diplomacy. Cooperation is structurally engrained in the inner workings of both the EU and ESA, being themselves the result of multilateral construction. It is perhaps for this reason that European stakeholders today maintain cooperative relations with almost all other space actors worldwide (Aliberti, 2015).

Because of this well-established network of cooperative activities with other global or regional powers, Europe is well positioned to utilize space to support its diplomatic objectives. Despite this, Europe lags somewhat behind such countries as the United States and China in leveraging this potential for political strategic purposes. To a large extent, this is because the European approach to international cooperation is not driven by a foreign policy agenda, but by programmatic opportunities, mostly in the ESA framework.[4]

However, with the progressive involvement of the EU in space matters, a broader strategy for international space relations might gradually emerge, driven by increasing synergy and complementarity among European constituencies. The development

[3]Copernicus and Galileo-related initiatives are for instance used to help spread the adoption and development of space-based solutions; competitions are held to incentivise researchers, entrepreneurs and start-ups in solving specific space applications challenges; and more than 15 ESA BICs provide support to develop space-based solutions and spinoffs.

[4]As "a European research and development organisation, ESA is a programmatically driven organisation i.e. the international cooperation is driven by programmatic needs more than a general "foreign policy" as is the case for Sovereign States" (Aliberti & Lisitsyna, 2019; Fonseca, 2013).

of a common European space diplomacy has been primarily led by the EU, which since the entry into force of the Lisbon Treaty in 2009 has taken primary responsibility for defining and representing the external dimensions of the European space programme (Aliberti, 2015). This has been duly reflected, for instance in the Space Dialogues the EC has set up with United States, Russia, China, Japan and South Africa to address a variety of civilian and security issues. In collaboration with its member states, the EU has also become actively involved in the work of international organisations and committees such as the International Telecommunication Union (ITU), the International Committee on Global Navigation Satellite Systems (ICG) and the UN COPUOS. Even more noticeable is the leading role played by the EU since 2007 in the preparation, negotiation and tentative adoption of an International Code of Conduct for Outer Space Activities (ICoC). Even though the original initiative ultimately failed to reach its objective, the EU and its member states demonstrated their willingness to move forward in the promotion of norms of responsible space behaviour to advance the safety, security, and sustainability of space activities.[5]

The European way of utilizing space for diplomatic purposes showcases Europe's interest in safeguarding international security stability (be it in space and on Earth) and addressing global challenges, such as those stemming from climate changes. In these contexts, European diplomatic initiatives and cooperative undertakings with third countries have been proliferating over the past years, making Europe a more credible interlocutor on the international stage. What is, perhaps, still missing in the promotion of a stronger and consistent 'European way' to space diplomacy is a higher degree of coordination with national space agencies, which conduct many international cooperation activities under their own steam, and which are central to strengthening Europe's weight in the international arena and multiplying its effectiveness in prosecuting foreign policy objectives.

With respect to the utilisation of space to enhance Europe's global standing and overall soft power, Europe still has a considerable amount of untapped potential, also in light of the cooperative nature of European space activities, their socio-economic focus, and the global reach that European programmes have. Despite its landmark achievements and the ground-breaking nature of many of its space endeavours, Europe has not been fully adept in turning space into a European tradition to be proud of, in making its citizens more aware of space as a true success story for Europe, and eventually in crafting strong domestic support for Europe's space efforts for the benefit of its overall global standing. Additionally, the impact of European space activities on citizens of other countries beyond Europe follows along the same line.

This is well evidenced by the non-existence of a "European space blockbuster" and, according to many, by the absence of an effective marketing strategy for the European space programme—something that European stakeholders are still less

[5]The European External Action Service declared in 2018 continuing European interest in bringing once again to international discussion the idea of adoption of a voluntary international instrument setting the rules of the road for responsible behaviour in space for countries engaging in space and aspiring to become spacefaring nations. This announcement stated that the new approach would be more closely pursued through a UN framework.

keen on compared to other space actors. In looking at current and foreseen developments in this respect, policy instruments in place and on the negotiating table at the European level do not suggest a dramatic turn of events. This applies both to the development of capacities more suited for soft power utilisation and to the missing marketing campaign for space.

Security and Defence

Regarding security and defence, Europe has been making use of space applications rather well, with space infrastructure now supporting multiple policies and activities within and outside European borders including, among others, civil protection and police missions, maritime security (e.g. traffic monitoring, surveillance of illegal activities, Search and Rescue missions), border surveillance and humanitarian aid (Moranta, Pavesi, Perrichon, Plattard, & Sarret, 2018).

Most programmes/capabilities are owned by individual European countries. However, following the adoption of Lisbon Treaty, which established a close link between space and the Union's Common Security and Defence Policy (CSDP), the EU has been increasingly emphasizing the use of space systems to enhance its security policies. Security in the EU is generally taken in a wider sense and covers not only military operations, but also the environment, energy and food security, early warning, crisis prevention and management, peacekeeping, civil protection and other areas (Aliberti & Lahcen, 2015).

Among other tasks, the EU's two flagship programmes, Copernicus and Galileo, have been developed to improve the management of security-related challenges, The Copernicus Service for Security (CSS) applications is designed to support European Union policies by providing information in response to Europe's security challenges (Copernicus Security Service, n.d.). The service improves crisis prevention, preparedness, and response in the three key areas of border surveillance (entrusted to FRONTEX); maritime surveillance (entrusted to the European Maritime Safety Agency—EMSA) and support to EU External Action (entrusted to the EU SatCen). Through the Copernicus Emergency Management and Security Services, Copernicus data are actively used at all stages of disaster management (i.e. prevention, preparedness, response and recovery) and support a variety of security operations conducted by national and European organisations inside and outside the EU.[6]

As for Galileo, the system is designed to address a range of security needs, including the provision of dedicated localisation and navigation services for troops and vehicles both on the ground and in the air. The European GNSS Agency (GSA) will also offer support to humanitarian search and rescue activities and will provide public authorities with encrypted signals as well as warnings if the signal's integrity is at

[6]Copernicus products and services are, for instance, used in the frame of assistance to third countries in situations of crisis, through peacekeeping operations, conflict prevention and resolution activities, as well as in risk assessment of global and trans-regional threats that might bring political destabilisation (Moranta et al., 2018).

risk. With regard to this last function, the GSA is undertaking security accreditation of the complete Galileo system, its operations and services, through an independent Security Accreditation Board (SAB).[7] Remarkably, the Galileo infrastructure also includes the Galileo Security Monitoring Centre (GSMC), which is responsible for monitoring and taking action regarding security threats and the operational status of the system components, managing Public Regulated Services (PRS) access on system level, implementing joint actions in case of crisis, and providing PRS and Galileo security expertise and analysis (Galileo Security Monitoring Centre, 2016).

Besides Copernicus and Galileo, the progression towards a stronger integration of space assets within Europe's security and defence policies is further evidenced by the more recent GOVSATCOM initiative, the inclusion of space in the implementation of the European Defence Action Plan and setting up of a European Defence Fund, as well as by the ongoing EC efforts to strengthen security requirements in developing and operating European space systems.[8]

This last effort, which comprises the various developments ongoing in the areas of cyber and space security—two increasingly important subsets of Europe's broader CSDP—stems from the recognition of the need to protect the EU's space infrastructure and hence secure the results of the continuous and substantial investment made by public and private actors in the space sector. Tacking stock of the growing societal dependence on space assets and of the great strategic value these assets have for security and defence purposes, the efforts to secure the services provided by the space infrastructure are part of the broader need to protect the European economy and society.

If it is clear that when compared to other major powers, much work remains to be done in harnessing the role of space within the security and, more crucially, defence realms, with the many ongoing developments at the EU level, a more robust European stance in these fields has started to take shape. The publication of the European Defence Action Plan and subsequent establishment of the European Defence Fund, the initiation of the Permanent Structured Cooperation frameworks and new security-related components of the Union's Space Programme (SSA, GOVSATCOM), all provide clear indications of an enhanced European profile in the field of security and military space activities.

All in all, even though Europe's focus has traditionally been more on socio-economic issues and initiatives, things have started shifting, and Europe is gradually providing itself with a more rich and complete set of capabilities across the whole spectrum of space initiatives, both in terms of hard capacities and, as just highlighted, soft capacities. This is visible and reflected in the scores obtained in the space power matrix, as Europe's overall capacity is second only to the United States.

---

[7]The SAB is in charge of verifying the compliance of the programme with the applicable security rules and regulations established by the Council and the European Commission, and of initiating and monitoring the implementation of security requirements to verify a high, robust and uniform level of security for EU GNSS systems (Moranta et al., 2018).

[8]In this context, the June 2018 European Commission's space regulation proposal aims to reinforce the GSA's mandate, increasing its responsibility for the security accreditation of all components of the EU space programmes.

4.1.2 … Lacking Autonomy

In spite of its wide array of capabilities, Europe at large fails to reach the same level of autonomy as its international partners or competitors. Remarkably, this is the case for both the technical and political dimensions of European autonomy over space matters.

4.1.2.1 The Issue of Technological Dependence

While Europe possesses the broad majority of the technologies, processes and industrial capabilities needed to develop space programmes, European stakeholders still need to externally source certain components, and raw and advanced materials as well as some basic technologies and building blocks that are not available within European boundaries (Caito, 2015). As shown in Table 4.2, several dependence situations can be identified within the European context.

The most evident example of European technological dependence is the number of foreign EEE components utilized in European satellites: the European Space Technology Master Plan (ESTMP) reports that "on a typical ESA satellite programme more than half of the EEE component procurement costs are still associated to components procured from outside Europe" (European Space Agency, European Commission, 2017). Remarkably, this is in stark contrast to the policies of "[t]he governments of the major space nations outside of the EU [which] are investing considerable amounts of money on EEE technologies to maintain access to key capabilities" (European Space Agency, European Commission, 2017, p. 20).

In addition to EEE components, there are many other technical domains where Europe relies on foreign sources for meeting critical needs, including, for instance,

Table 4.2 Scenarios of technological dependence

Technology unavailable in Europe at all	Need to procure from elsewhere, without any other relevant alternative in the short-term. This translates to a weak bargaining position and unavoidable dependence on the will of those who procure the technology
Technology available but with inappropriate level of maturity, reliability and/or cost	Less critical but still prevailing rationale to procure from elsewhere. The other option is to use the locally available technology but with lower performance, greater risk, and less flexible time predictions
Technology available but needs to be replaced because it will become unavailable	No short-term risk of unavailability, but need to procure technologies elsewhere because the technology is becoming obsolete, does not meet new legal standards or will be no longer produced by the supplier

advanced materials, equipment, processes, and modelling tools. In short, European technical/technological dependence is a wide-encompassing issue, with the extent of this dependence spanning from the specific satellite technological subsystems to the more generic components that can be integrated transversally among multiple systems and architectures. To this, one needs to add eventual lack or low level of capacities that are nevertheless necessary to the conduct of space activities (say SSA or manned space), the reliance on some critical items (such as the Ukrainian-built upper stage for the Vega launcher), or entire systems (such as the Russian-made Soyuz launcher), as well as critical data (such as, most notably, Europe's reliance on U.S. data for SSA or intelligence, surveillance and reconnaissance—ISR).

All this clearly places Europe in a position of strong dependence. It is important to highlight, however, that the most worrisome aspect is not Europe's reliance on final products, but rather on basic technologies, since the lower the level of technology on which a country or region is dependent, the greater the weakness of the country or region (Caito, 2015).

Finding itself in the state of technological dependence equals having a restricted access to state-of-the-art technologies and an incomplete traceability and visibility of the supply chain. The technological dependence consequently leads to several considerable negative impacts. An illustrative list of these ramifications is provided in Fig. 4.2.

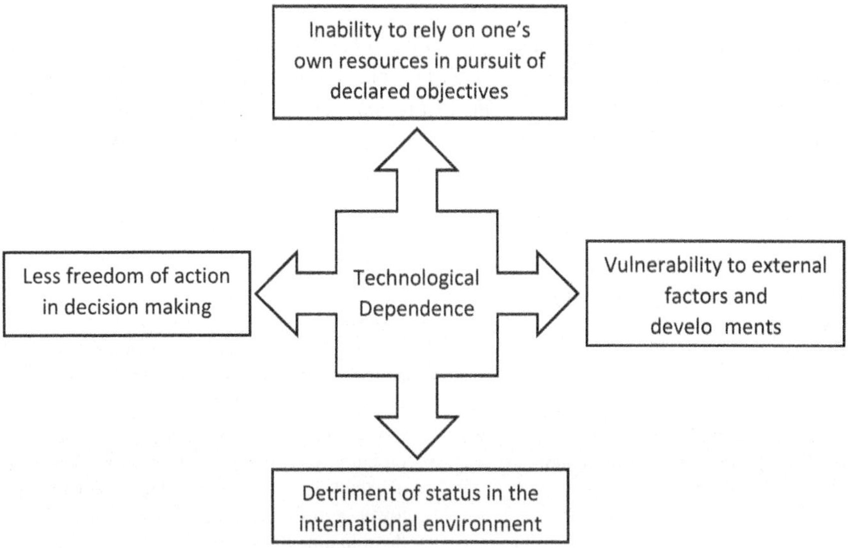

Fig. 4.2 Impacts of technological dependence

Non-dependence Initiatives

The progressive recognition that Europe's high level of dependence can potentially undermine any European space activities has led European decision-makers to kick-start a number of initiatives to address the issue. An overview of these activities is provided in Fig. 4.3.

The first notable communitarian effort was initiated by ESA in 2000, with the launch of the Space Technology Harmonisation Process. This process aimed to "achieve better-coordinated research and development (R&D) activities among all actors of European space sector and to establish a strong technology base as key to the worldwide competitiveness of European industry and to the success of future space missions" (European Space Agency, European Commission, 2017, p. 24).

As the harmonisation process advanced, more technology roadmaps were developed—as illustrated by Table 4.3—and many additional organizations started becoming involved. Today, the initiative "includes ESA Member States, the European Cooperating States (ECS), the European Commission (EC), the European Defence Agency (EDA), Eurospace, SME4Space, industry and research organisations" (European Space Agency, European Commission, 2017, p. 26).

Within ESA, the recognition of the dependence of Europe's space sector on non-European components suppliers resulted in the creation of the European Component Initiative (ECI). The initiative (initially formulated as the EEE Parts European Action

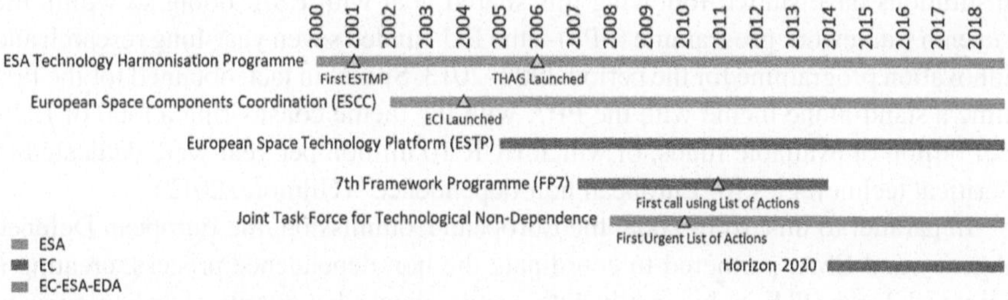

Fig. 4.3 European-level initiatives to foster non-dependence

Table 4.3 Harmonised roadmaps and roadmap activities, 2001–2016

Harmonised roadmaps and roadmap activities since 2001 as of 31.12.2016	
Total number of harmonisation roadmap activities	6265
Total number of roadmaps	129
Number of cycles	31
Revisits	47
Total budget (million EUR)	4370
Average activity budget (thousand EUR)	696

Source European Space Agency, European Commission (2017)

Plan) is an open cooperative project with ESA and partner national space agencies each participating with their own funding. The implementation of ECI has taken place in four phases, with the latest (Phase 4) covering the period 2013–2017. As a result of the initiative and the activities led by the European Space Components Coordination (ESCC)—a supplementary formed body representing all major stakeholders from component manufacturers to prime contractors—three key reference lists have been published and updated (QPL—ESCC Qualified Parts List, QML—ESCC Qualified Manufacturers List, and EPPL—European Preferred Parts List) to meet the Initiative's primary goal to maintain and enhance a European industrial base for critical technologies needed by Europe's space missions. However, due to the uneven motivation of ESA Member States to invest in technological non-dependence and the high degree of concentration of the EEE components industry within a handful of countries, the initiative ultimately failed to reach its objectives in the ESA framework, paving the way for a complementary action under the umbrella of the EU, which seemed more appropriate.

Indeed, with the eventual involvement of the EU in space matters during the 2000s, additional initiatives towards technological non-dependence were kick-started. As ESA and EU tied their relations with the EU-ESA framework agreement, the ensuing European space policy jointly formulated and accepted in 2007 acknowledged the pursuit of European industrial non-dependence from international suppliers of critical components as a key European goal. In this way, non-dependence became explicitly linked to the harmonisation process, and since 2007 the European Union and its institutions have started following this shared goal with ESA, doing so within the seventh framework programme (FP7)—the EU-funded seven year-long research and innovation programme for the period 2007–2013. Space, in fact, obtained for the first time a stand-alone theme with the FP7, with the theme considering a total of EUR 1.4 billion of available funds, of which EUR 10 million per year were dedicated to "critical technologies for European non-dependence" (Gilmore, 2012).

In parallel to this, from 2008, the European Commission, the European Defence Agency and ESA, partnered to coordinate the non-dependence process, creating a joint task force (JTF) to biennially define and review a list of critical technologies to be developed to foster non-dependence in space (see Box 1).

Box 1 Prioritising Investments in Critical Technologies

Within the European context, the word *critical technologies* is generally used to indicate those *technologies that enable Europe to be capable of responding to its own needs in space and to remain competitive in the global market.* Clearly, identifying the level of criticality and setting the level of priority to be assigned to the various actions is not a straightforward exercise, as it requires the harmonisation of the perspectives and preferences of different stakeholders. From an institutional perspective, a technology may be critical because it addresses critical applications, from an industrial perspective, a technology may be considered critical because its supply availability is critical.

Although there is still an ongoing debate on what perspective should be given priority, an extensive list of technologies that are not available in Europe has been defined by the JTF through consultation with all relevant stakeholders. These consultations have allowed to gather feedback from Member States, Industry and SMEs and consolidate inputs in a list of actions that reflects the consensus on the Critical Space Technologies for European Strategic Non-Dependence. The criteria used to evaluate if a technology can be included in the final list of actions are:

1. Items shall be of low integration level, i.e. building blocks and components (System/sub-system assembly, methods are not included)
2. Items shall have a clearly identified function and performance target
3. Items shall be multi use and/or applications (i.e. not an enabling technology for a one shot use)
4. Items shall be not available from a European source and for which the unrestricted
5. availability from non-European suppliers cannot be assured
6. Critical items for which no adequate or sufficient action is on-going (European Commission, 2017).

Building upon the established list of technologies, the JTF has established a methodology for the selection of the actions to be potentially funded through the EU Framework Programmes. Within H2020, the selection is based upon the appraisal of the 43 actions from the list of critical technologies with respect to three main criteria:

1. *Policy relevance*: adherence of the action with the "Space Strategy for Europe", adopted by the European Commission in 2016;
2. *Programmatic fit*: suitability of the H2020 grants in implementing the action from a programmatic perspective, including budget, timeline and Technology Readiness Level;
3. *Consistency with on-going or planned activities*: continuation potential complementarity with respect to past or on-going activities in EU or ESA and risk of duplication/overlapping with on-going or planned FP7/H2020 projects.

The three main criteria of equal importance are further broken down into a set of specific sub-criteria with associated metrics. With respect to the relevant metrics, each action is ranked reflecting its level of compliance with the sub-criterion. For each main criterion, ranks of the relevant sub-criteria are combined in accordance to predefined logics into an overall appraisal of the action. Filtering the actions with respect to the appraisal flags finally results into the short list of selected actions (European Commission, 2017).

The last edition (JTF List of Actions 2018–2020) was released in 2016 and targets the years 2018–2020. On the basis of this list a dedicated Horizon 2020 topic

Table 4.4 JTF list of actions 2018–2020

Group A (2018)	Group B (2019)	Group C (2020)
• High capacity FPGAs • ASICS: 28 nm deep sub-micron • Active discrete power components • RF components • Passive components • High temperature packaging	• ASICS for mixed signal processing • Design and qualification of μcontroller for space applications • Design and prototype of nvRAM for SPACE with serial interface • High density (1000 pins and beyond) assembly capabilities and PCBs • Photonics components • Advanced laser crystals for high power space applications	• Very high performance microprocessors • Design and prototype of ultra-reprogrammable SoCs • Fibre optic or photonic integrated technology gyro-based inertial measurement unit (IMU) • Power amplification: travelling wave tube materials • SW tool: automatic generation of code • Advanced materials and material technology for combustion chambers

was established in the H2020 Work Programme 2018–2020 titled "Technologies for European non-dependence and competitiveness"[9] (European Commission, 2018d) with an indicative budget of EUR 36 million divided into three annual call for project proposals requesting a contribution from the EU of between EUR 1 and 3 million. The topic description reaffirms the need for European autonomy by arguing that "Europe needs non-dependent access to critical space technologies, which is a *sine qua non* condition for achieving Europe's strategic objectives" (European Commission, 2018d, p. 32, 33).

With the first call for applications closed in March 2018 and next two expecting completion in 2019 and 2020, the SPACE-10-TEC-2018-2020 will ensure sequential implementation of actions identified in the JTF List of Actions 2018–2020 (Table 4.4).

Concerning upcoming developments, a dedicated Joint Technology Initiative (JTI) for space is envisioned to be set-up in the next framework programme. Similar to other existing JTIs in other industrial sectors, the European Commission will set up a JTI in the form of a public–private partnership with support from ASD Eurospace.

Overall, the creation of multiple harmonisation roadmaps, the coordination of parallel programmes by EU, ESA, member states and various stakeholders, the constant monitoring and update of technological priorities, all show that Europe is trying to address the problem of technological dependence. But is autonomy the ultimate objective?

[9]In a similar fashion to this latest development, the JTF published such list of actions already in previous years and this was similarly translated into Horizon 2020 topics in the 2014–2015 and 2016–2017 Work Programmes under the title "COMPET-1: Technologies for European non-dependence and competitiveness".

Autonomy: Not the Ultimate Objective!

When looking at all the above-described European actions in the field of technological development, it clearly emerges that they are primarily driven by the resolve to avoid growing dependency on non-European sources, avoid cases of worldwide unique sources through international cooperation, and promote greater security of supply. The overarching objective is hence to ensure the possibility for European industry to have unrestricted access to the state-of-the-art in all space-related technologies, independent from broader sovereignty considerations put forward at governmental level.

Admittedly, the situation has substantially improved over the past 20 years. To illustrate, the ratio of European to non-European EEE-parts has significantly increased. In 2015, 50% of the part types (in terms of value) were procured from European suppliers, compared to just 15% in 2000. In addition, Europe's dependence upon suppliers in the U.S. has been further reduced by 8% through coordination with JAXA (European Space Agency, European Commission, 2017).

However, it does not go unnoticed that the gap remains too big for Europe to achieve technological self-reliance (Caito, 2015), at least in the short run. Similarly, the mechanisms put in place are not appropriate to achieving this goal. ESA and EC's technology programmes are certainly good steps in this direction, but they are mainly focused on developing preliminary concepts with a Low Technology Readiness Level (TRL). The key issues of maturation, testing and in-orbit qualification of critical technologies, are not fully covered, leaving industry to bear the financial burdens and risks of qualification of the technologies they demand.[10] And while industry is certainly interested in enlarging the technological portfolio, it cannot and will not invest in the development of new technologies "just" for the sake of sovereignty. Clearly, this should be the role of public institutions. However, European institutions have shied away from shouldering the burden associated with the development of critical technologies, choosing instead to invest in the development of technologies and systems that bring quick returns on investment (European Space Policy Institute, 2017).

In the final analysis, what becomes clear is that "a substantial level of dependence—mostly on U.S. suppliers—has been accepted in many areas where no economic rationale can justify the investment. Such de facto acceptance of strong reliance on non-domestic sources is a European particularity. This is most likely deeply rooted in European culture, which is much more prone to international cooperation than to international competition" (Tortora, 2015, p. 166).

Europeans are fully aware that situations of critical dependency create evident constraints, primarily in the form of delays and over-costs that hamper productivity and market competitiveness. However, as aptly put by Tortora "these constraints have not deemed sufficient to justify the investment, because the limited size of the markets to be potentially addressed with such technologies" (Therefore) "unlike all the other

---

[10]The same EC Framework Programmes, which were explicitly devised to translate research into marketable goods, are not apposite because of the co-funding obligations for the European industry.

space faring nations for which national autonomy and sovereignty are sufficient justifications in themselves for public expenditures made in this area, European public investments in space are primarily subject to direct economic return" (Tortora, 2015, p. 166). This represents another unique feature of the current European approach to space, a feature that has cast a shadow over Europe's ability to deal with the hard cases of the development of critical technologies that do not have a clear return on investment in the commercial market.

Two caveats must be underlined in this context:

- At the onset of Europe's journey into space, efforts in the field were primarily driven by political rather than economic considerations. This is, for instance, well evidenced by the very decision to develop an indigenous European means of accessing space, following the well-known refusal of the U.S. to launch the French-German Symphonie satellites. Yet, quite ironically, it was in that very initial stage of politically-set decisions that the logic of commercial gains became deeply entrenched in the European approach to space. This can be mainly explained by the remarkable success of Ariane on the open market of launch services, as well as the key position that the European space industry has gained on the telecommunications satellites commercial market. Because of the lack of a key anchor customer for European industry and the overall limited size of European institutional demand, this success has indeed enabled Europe to amortize the fixed costs for the development of its institutional programme "while achieving strategic goals as a positive externality without paying the full price" (European Space Policy Institute, 2019).
- There are visible differences between European actors, the most prominent being between France and Germany. While the former has been often prone to space-related investment on pure political grounds, the latter has conversely championed an economic-driven approach. The views expressed in the June 2018 Proposal for the establishment of the EU Space Programme are also evidence of this divergence in mind-set.

It is beyond the scope of this study to engage in detail such issues, but it is necessary to highlight that these divergences underscore an even more crucial aspect of Europe's autonomy (or lack thereof)—the political dimension.

4.1.2.2 The Lack of Political Autonomy

As a complicated tangle of different interests and institutions, Europe's political autonomy in space can be (and has been) questioned.

Although the existence of a *European actorness* is widely acknowledged, it is also clear that Europe is not a state-nation in a Westphalian sense, nor has a polity emerged from a single, authoritative source as in other countries.[11] It is a *unicum*

[11] According to the definition of William Wallace, the EU can be regarded as a "partial, multi-layered polity", that is a "political entity which lacks, however, many of the features that one might expect to find in a traditional state" (Wallace, 2005).

on the international stage, by virtue of its status as something more than an intergovernmental organisation but less than a fully-fledged European 'state' (Hill & Smith, 2005, p. 4). Many debates and much analysis have been produced through the years in the attempt to understand what particular kind of actor the EU is and what implications this actorness brings. As remarkably pointed out by Henry Kissinger:

> Europe represents in some sense a renunciation of Westphalia, or alternatively, its transformation into a new international system based on regional, not national, units. "The outcome has combined aspects of both national and regional approaches without, as yet, securing the full benefits of either. The EU diminishes its Member States' sovereignty and traditional government functions, such as control of their currency and borders. On the other hand, European politics remains primarily national, and in many countries, objections to the EU policies have become the central domestic issue. The result is a hybrid, constitutionally something between a state and a confederation, operating through ministerial meetings and a common bureaucracy… Yet, the EU struggles to resolve its internal tensions in the quest for the principles and goals by which it is guided. In the process, it pursues monetary union side by side with fiscal dispersion and bureaucracy at odds with democracy. In foreign policy it embraces universal ideals without the means to enforce them, and a cosmopolitan identity in contention with national loyalties – with European unity accompanied by east-west and north-south divides and an ecumenical attitude toward autonomy movements (Catalan, Bavarian, Scot) challenging the integrity of States". In short, the EU can be seen as a hybrid of contending aspirations and contradictory trends. (Kissinger, 2014, p. 92, 93)

Understandably, this peculiar status is fully reflected in the space realm, with a number of negative consequences on both the internal and external dimension of Europe's political sovereignty over space matters.

The Internal Dimension of Political Autonomy

Although from an industrial perspective the European space sector is much more advanced than any other industrial sector in terms of integration, from a political perspective the sector is characterised by fragmentation. As discussed in Chap. 1, European space governance remains a function of the interaction between three distinct constituencies, which creates a triangular governance structure. At the one tip there are the different member states and their national space agencies that are mainly committed to conducting space activities in the interests of their own countries rather than of Europe as a whole. At the second tip there is ESA, an intergovernmental organisation, *regional*, which over the past 40 years has taken the lead in crafting the concept of a regional (not national nor supranational) space agency, carrying out the major European space endeavours and strengthening the European space identity, though lacking a political clout. At the third tip there is the EU, which since the 2000s has started to position itself as an additional and effective space player, demonstrating the willingness—and in a sense the legitimacy—to complement ESA's actions with political leadership in a few given programmatic areas. Each player in this composition has its own competences and interests.[12] More importantly, the interplay between national, intergovernmental and communitarian frameworks has created institutional misalignment, making decision-making processes inherently cumbersome.

The very formulation of "national interest" in such a framework is not a straightforward exercise as it requires the ability to strike an appropriate balance between the priorities of individual member states as well as the harmonisation of different responsibilities and procedures among European institutions. As also stressed by Algieri, "defining a common policy in such a system is a complex and interwoven process of formulating interests and decision-making rules that span over different levels, i.e. the supranational, the national and the subnational one. Different actors with specific interests cooperate horizontally (between the institutions of the EU as well as between the Member States) and vertically (between the supranational, national and subnational level) to commonly agree on problem solving mechanisms and to use them" (Algieri, 2015).

Because of this tangle of relationships, institutions, and multi-level sharing of competences, Europe as a whole lacks the core features defining domestic sovereignty over space matters[13]: i.e. autonomy in decision-making and effective control over policy implementation.

With regard to the former aspect, pan-European institutions still struggle to have *de jure* and de facto autonomy to determine policies. In terms of formal authority, it can be noted that not every space-related field is a European-level competence. Defence issues, for instance, mostly remain the domain of the Member States. According to Art. 189 of the Lisbon Treaty, the European Union can implement space policies "to promote scientific and technical progress, industrial competitiveness and the implementation of its policies". These competences, however, are not exclusive,[14]

[12]ESA is not an Agency of the European Union. ESA and the EU are separate institutions: ESA is an inter-governmental organisation, while the EU is supranational. The two institutions have different ranges of competences, different member states and are governed by different rules and procedures. While the EU was founded to enhance political, economic and social cooperation among member states, which have for these reasons set up common institutions to which they delegate some of their sovereignty, "ESA was more the result of a coordinated European space effort from scientists". The main objective, as underlined by the Convention, was to create an international organisation, pooling the resources of European countries to enable scientists to make a valuable contribution to the exploration and study of outer space.

[13]"Domestic sovereignty refers to the formal organization of political authority within the state and the ability of public authorities to exercise effective control within the borders of their own polity" (Krasner, 1999, p. 4).

[14]According to Art. IV of the Treaty on the Functioning of the European Union (TFEU), space (together with internal market, regional policy (cohesion), agriculture and fisheries, environment, consumer protection, transport, energy, research and few other areas) falls under the "shared competences", in which both the EU and EU countries are able to legislate and adopt legally binding acts. The other main types of competencies within the EU according to the TFEU are exclusive competencies (in which the EU alone is able to legislate and adopt binding acts) and supporting competencies (in which the EU can only intervene to support, coordinate or complement the action of EU countries).

meaning that member states are free to manage programmes domestically, through unilateral, bilateral or multilateral initiatives, irrespective of (and possibly also in conflict with) European-set policies.

The problem is, however, more fundamental than the existence of "parallel" authority structures at European level. In fact, even when European institutions are endowed with formal authority, the de facto power to define pan-European policies has ultimately remained in the hands of the various national entities. As a result, for the implementation of their space projects, both the EU and ESA are ultimately dependent on a "green light" from their member states—an aspect that can, in turn, slow down (or even undermine) the development of major European initiatives and ultimately impair Europe's ability to develop a clear and coherent strategy for the future. In addition, much work remains to be done in the definition of the respective roles of ESA and the EU, and coordination with national agencies. At present, the relationship between the EU and ESA has remained a rather complex one. Such complexity not only stems from the different nature of the institutions, but also from the fact that the two organisations have different ranges of competences, different member states, and are governed by different rules and procedures.

Inevitably, the scattered distribution of competences, the lack of effective power and the exposure to interference from constituents and concurrent interests all result in a relatively low executive autonomy. Because of the need to achieve consensus among the different national, intergovernmental, and communitarian interests as well as the need to strike a balance between the distinctive procurement and industrial policies, the implementation of European space policies is neither agile nor straightforward, especially when compared to other major space nations. This is also the case when it comes to the enactment of well-understood and shared European interests, such as the need for clear procurement rules for European programmes. The clearest example is that of launchers, with less than one third of European owned/operated satellites launched with a European rocket. However, the concept applies to the whole space value chain. How can policy-makers adopt policies and decisions for Europe and expect them to be implemented if even national governments decide to fly on the cheapest carrier or to buy foreign solutions rather than relying on European ones?

One such situation is in stark contrast to the posture of all other space nations—be they the United States, Russia, China, Japan or India—and greatly contributes to undermining the actual level of political autonomy of European institutions. In short, because "Europe's many voices and often conflicting national interests [continue to] significantly weaken its ability to act in a cohesive let alone sustained manner" (Schubert, 2015), a great deal of intra-European work remains be done to really empower common institutions with effective authority. In this context, a cooperation mechanism at the head-of-state level may be required to reconcile differing national priorities and preferences and ensure pan-European coherence.

The External Dimension of Political Autonomy

The external dimension of European autonomy over space matters can also be questioned. Certainly, Europe as a whole enjoys international legal sovereignty as well as a degree of Westphalian sovereignty, in the sense that it is a polity premised on the exclusion of external actors from internal authority arrangements (Krasner, 1999). The autonomy and mandate for "external action" of the EU has been further strengthened with the entry into force of the Lisbon Treaty, which put in place more consistent institutional arrangements, including the creation of the positions of the President of the European Council and the High Representative for Foreign Affairs and Security Policy (HR). Supported by the European External Action Service, the HR manages EU's diplomatic relations with third-countries and develops common external policies in a broad range of foreign policy fields (including space), thus establishing Europe as a reliable, capable and autonomous international actor.

In spite of these praiseworthy developments, Europe's autonomy on the international scene remains somewhat impaired by two sources of dependency: internal and external. Internal factors derive from the multi-layered institutional framework already discussed. Even though the institutional arrangements under the Lisbon Treaty have offered, new tools to promote the consistency of all external activities as well as coherence between external and "internal" EU action, the reality is that "the EU does not, as yet, possess full strategic independence" (Robinson, 2011; Algieri, 2015): insofar as it is up to the Member States to define the common path forward, Europe will but remain a restricted foreign political actor in the international stage.

Externally, European autonomy is affected by a number of factors. These factors first include its exceedingly complex state of interdependence within the international system. It is widely acknowledged that "the process of foreign policy-making of a state cannot be developed by disrespecting the interests and strategies of other states as well as the institutional obligations deriving from participation in multilateral organisations" (Algieri, 2015).

Beyond interdependence, Europe's external sovereignty is impaired by its exposure to foreign interventions and invitations—i.e. "voluntary policies that compromise the autonomy of their own polity" (Krasner, 1999). With regard to the former, European stakeholders are subject to different forms of coercion (a situation in which one state threatens to impose sanctions on another if the target state does not alter its policies), and impositions (a situation in which the target state has no choice but to accept the demands of the initiator). A tangible example is the technology transfer requirements implied by the ITAR, which have de facto created an international embargo based on U.S. export licences (Mineiro, 2011), also for Europeans. Given that many European space systems include critical U.S. components, it can be argued that the U.S. essentially has a veto power over European decision-making autonomy vis-à-vis external actors. This has proved to be the case of several European cooperation activities with third countries, such as India and China. To be sure, since the late 1990s several European countries and companies have made increasing efforts to develop an ITAR-free business model for the manufacture of commercial satellites (Zhao & Bian, 2011), and, as discussed above, efforts are being made to achieve strategic non-dependence in key technologies. The underlying issue, however, remains broader than just loosening this dependency or circumventing legal obstacles.

An analysis of the broader European space relations with foreign actors clearly shows how sensitive Europeans are about U.S. preferences. This "sensitivity" ultimately points to the fundamental structural weakness in Europe's space diplomacy, namely the current pan-European inability to advance its own space agenda when it directly affects U.S. interests and security concerns (Aliberti, 2015). Taking into account the long-lasting transatlantic partnership, European institutions have often accepted impositions from the U.S. that have forced Europe to voluntarily constrain its actions and policies. This situation was, for instance, evidenced by the decision halt cooperation with China during the early stages of the development of the Galileo constellation following U.S. diplomatic pressure. The reasons behind such stance are manifold, but a crucial aspect is the dependencies deriving from the historical and institutional settings of European integration: as long as member states are responsible for any final decision and as long as they conduct their own foreign policies and diplomatic alignments with one or more foreign countries, Europe will remain but vulnerable to foreign interests targeting single member states to undermine a European consensus (i.e. through a *divide and conquer* strategy). Clearly, this is a highly critical issue that undermines European external autonomy—be it in space or any other sector—more than any other established powerhouse.

4.1.3 What Kind of Actor?

The considerations provided thus far underpin the conclusion that Europe cannot be considered a full-fledged "space power". The main evidence supporting this claim is the evident mismatch between Europe's high level of capacity and its low level of autonomy, with this latter dimension single-handedly preventing Europe from falling within the "space powers" quadrant.

Admittedly, its present position within the matrix is close to reaching the space power quadrant, a target that might be achieved in a reasonable timeframe, provided that proper processes are implemented (see Box 2). In principle, it may therefore be agreed that Europe can be considered a "space power in the making" rather than a spacefaring "nation". This is consistent, for instance, with the views expressed by the European External Action Service.

Box 2 Quo Vadis Europe?

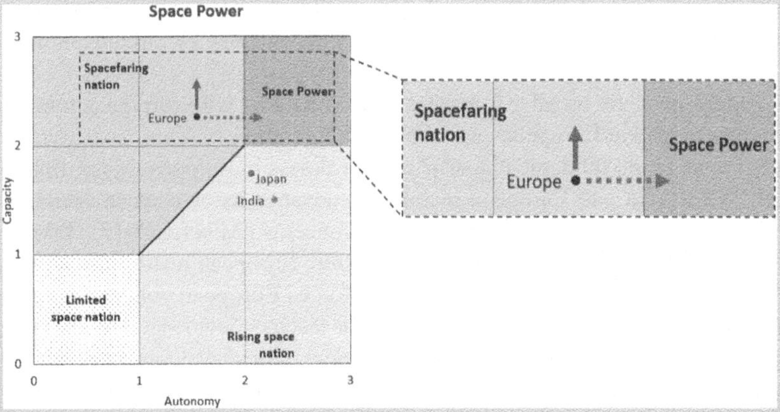

Taking into account unfolding and foreseen developments in Europe's space efforts, an upward movement in the capacity axis (brown arrow) could be expected as a result of increasing budgetary allocation to upgrade existing programmes and develop new ones (e.g. SST, GOVSATCOM). It is, however, important to stress that these evolutions will not automatically translate into an equally important rightward movement that would allow Europe to cross the space power threshold.

In fact, moving rightward on the autonomy axis (red arrow) would require dedicated efforts to tackle the lingering issue of dependency in its two constituent dimensions: technological and political. Some of the above discussed developments (i.e. the setting up of a dedicated Joint Technology Initiative (JTI) for space in the next framework programme) may contribute to this movement. It is however evident that even if that effort enables Europe to formally cross the space power threshold as defined by the theoretical framework, the gap that currently exists between Europe's overall level of autonomy and that of other space powers will remain well in place. This implies that if a decision to proactively pursue space power status is to be made, it should take into account the existing gaps and make the best possible effort to bridge them substantially and not just cosmetically.

However, there is still no concrete evidence to support this assertion. A first element confuting this progression is the above-discussed sensitivity of Europe to the issue of autonomy and its business-oriented approach, for they produce an evident discrepancy between Europe's claimed ambition to assert itself a space power and the financial, infrastructure and policy means to fulfil this objective. This is, for instance, reflected in the lack of definite procurement rules for institutional satellites and launch services that would prevent European industry from relying on non-European suppliers, and the limited funding provided to key initiatives such as ESA's European Component Initiative (ECI) and the Commission's calls in FP7 or Horizon 2020 frameworks. These lead to questions about the validity of objectives, implementation tools and, eventually, the strategic effectiveness. Nevertheless, some unfolding and praiseworthy developments—such as the introduction of a "buy European clause" in the June 2018 proposal for the establishment of the EU programme, the prospective budgetary boost for the next MFF,[15] and the announced creation of a European Innovation Council (EIC) and European Space Council (see below)—may greatly contribute to tackling this lingering issue.

However, a second, and more fundamental element is the still limited appetite of member states to consider strategic power in regard to European integration, be it in space or elsewhere. When looking at the underlying rationales that have led European countries to set up common institutions to which they delegate some of their sovereignty, considerations of power hardly feature as a primary objective. In fact, the nature of European integration has for long been revolving around economic rather than strategic considerations. As also explained in this context by Algieri:

> A major reason for the lack of an appropriate strategic profile is the reluctance of EU member states to commonly define their strategic interests, including agreement on operational steps that would need to be taken in the framework of the Common Foreign and Security Policy (CFSP) including the Common Security and Defence Policy (CSDP), in order to defend these interests. Learning lessons from European integration history, it becomes clear that the invitation to take part in deeper political integration including security and defence political integration is seen rather sceptically by sovereign EU member states who are more concerned about an erosion of their autonomy to take decisions in the field of high politics.

This issue has become even more pronounced over the past few years, with the rise of the so-called populist movements throughout Europe that have been challenging the political dimensions of European integration. As recently noted by Mario Draghi, president of the European Central Bank, "this tension between economic integration and political cooperation is fuelled by a powerful belief that there is an inherent trade-off between EU membership and the ability of countries to exercise sovereignty" (Draghi, 2019).

Although some new initiatives revolving around a communitarian approach to security and defence have been gradually put in place, particularly so in recent years (e.g. EU Global Strategy, PESCO, EDAP, EDF), the overarching paradigm has not drastically moved towards the establishment of Europe as a strong security and defence actor. In this context, the very issues behind the possible emergence of Europe as a military power and as a space power starkly converge: as long as member states are unwilling to revisit the overarching paradigm guiding European integration towards a more politically-driven approach in key issue-areas, there should be no expectations about its progression towards the (space) power status.

In conclusion, Europe's business-oriented approach, its de facto acceptance of its state of dependency, and its limited taste for international competition and power

[15] As of February 2019 (European Commission, 2018a).

considerations make it a *unicum* in the international arena, and ultimately raise the question whether Europe should ambition to set itself as a full-fledged space power or should rather limit its ambitions to being a spacefaring "nation", although among the most powerful ones, and adapt its strategy accordingly. In any case, European space policy should aim to avoid that this singularity turns into a weakness.

4.2 Should Europe Become a Full-Fledged Space Power?

Considering Europe's position within the space power matrix, answering the question of whether Europe should become a space power means answering the question of whether it is in Europe's interest to ensure that its great capacities are endowed with an appropriate level of autonomy in its two dimensions—technological and political. To answer this, a proper assessment of the stakes associated with the pursuit of autonomy is required.

4.2.1 Untangling the Stakes

As discussed in Sect. 2.3, there are security, economic and political stakes associated with pursuing, achieving and maintaining space power status. It is useful therefore to analyse Europe's possible pursuit of space autonomy in the light of these stakes; assess what Europe could gain by becoming a full-fledged space power and what Europe could miss out on or even lose (in a comparative perspective) by remaining a spacefaring actor[16]; and eventually indicate whether it is in Europe's interest to pursue space power status, thus placing certain stakes above others.

4.2.1.1 Economic Stakes

As already stressed, Europe's approach to space has been constructed around the ability of space to support public policies and European industries, while generating a substantial return on investments. Socio-economic considerations for investing

[16]In fact, the question to whether pursue the space power status or not has to take into account not only the benefits but also the potential losses coming from not doing so in the light of the highly competitive international environment characterising space activities. In fact, it is true that Europe is currently well endowed with a fairly large number of hard and soft capacities, thus potentially not being interested in further fostering its role by becoming space power. It is also true, however, that losses in absolute and relative terms alike would increase over time, as other actors keep progressing, developing more capacities that Europe not only could need but would also be dependent from, while losing ground in terms of what it can offer worldwide.

in space are thus of fundamental importance to any assessment of Europe's future path, as these will most probably continue to represent the overarching theme of its presence in space.

In looking at the economic stakes associated with the conduct of space activities, it can be noted that Europe has been already harvesting and benefiting extensively from these. Additional economic benefits and returns on investment do not necessarily stem from the pursuit of technological autonomy. This is especially so when it comes to the development of critical technologies that do not have a sufficient level of recurrent use on the commercial markets, because of the specificities of the space sector, namely demanding requirements, limited volumes, and cutting-edge technologies.

Clearly, this is not to downplay the different economic risks that Europe faces by maintaining the *status quo*. In fact, relying on sources outside Europe creates complications for European industry in terms of communication and quality control, and also introduces more risks with respect to the sustainability of supply. Reliance on components developed outside Europe can result "in longer lead times, increased costs and the potential non-availability for some European satellite manufacturers to high end technologies and or the detailed knowledge to use the technologies in the most optimal way" (European Space Agency, European Commission, 2017). The lack of access to leading edge technologies inevitably produces limitations on the performance and output of European systems, which directly affects the competitiveness of European industry (Caito, 2015). Besides affecting the cost and level of performance of industrial production and generating cost over-runs, dependency may also put on-time deliveries are at risk, because of the "cumbersome paperwork to be performed, as well as the highly variable implementation of export control regulations" (Tortora, 2015).

Nevertheless, from an economic standpoint, what is critical for European industry is not technological autonomy *tout court*—i.e. ensuring that all needed space technologies are developed in Europe—but rather non-dependence—i.e. ensuring the possibility of having unrestricted access to state-of-the art technologies. While self-reliance is obviously the most secure way to achieve non-dependence, this objective can be attained through more economically viable options, including diversification of the sources of supply and long-term political agreements with suppliers that guarantee access to any required technology and ensure the sustainability of supply. As explained by Caito, this is because "the mechanisms driving technology in the direction of short-term competitiveness and commercial programmes are profoundly different from those driving technology for strategic reasons, such as autonomy. Naturally, strategic actions will also have an impact, directly or indirectly, on the space economy and commercial activities, yet the return on investment will materialise only late in the process, and might not be directly traceable to the original investment" (Caito, 2015).

In short, from a pure economic perspective, moving to the right from spacefaring status to the space power status does not necessarily give rise to compelling economic incentives for European stakeholders. The key stakes for Europe's possible pursuit of autonomy are rather to be found in the security and political dimensions of space activities.

4.2.1.2 Security Stakes

From a security perspective, no actor with a minimum of strategic ambition in space can stand the consequences of a high level of dependence. This is equally true for Europe, even though the continent has, so far, tolerated a significant level of dependence on foreign technologies.

One of the most evident threats that Europe has to face by remaining a "spacefaring region" is supply insecurity. In fact, even with possible political agreements with foreign suppliers, Europe's condition of dependency will continue to expose it to many different risks and potential uncertainties. Europe, for instance, may be vulnerable to political instability, changing economic conditions or even a natural disaster in a supplier country. Security of supply may be threatened not only by political crisis and natural calamity, but also by the ever-changing regulatory barriers of export controls. Because the dual-use and highly sensitive nature of most space technologies implies their subjection to export restrictions as strategic and defence-related items, the risk is that some of them may in the future become completely unavailable from exporters, or subject to even more burdensome procurement delays that can have serious effects on European space programmes.

In this respect, a major inherent risk is that a foreign supplier could impose unacceptable conditions on providing technologies—particularly military ones—or even refuse to provide them on the basis of political considerations. The American initial opposition to the Galileo programme because of its military implications offers a clear case in point. This well-known episode also shows how Europe's lack of autonomy constantly risks being translated into programmatic insecurity and eventually impair policy implementation. In fact, should a supplier country raise objections to the final aim of a given European space programme, decision-makers would be forced to either implement a given programme without using the specific (would-be-optimal) technologies or to discontinue the programme altogether. From a security standpoint, this is not acceptable.

Another inherent risk associated with Europe's present condition lies in the difficulty of upholding security requirements throughout the value chain. This risk is well evidenced by "the rights awarded to suppliers' national authorities through the implementation of export control regulations. As a matter of fact, in order to achieve full visibility and transparency on the final use of the critical components at stake, European companies are required to fully open their books and to grant unlimited access to their facilities to foreign authorities. This is fair and acceptable in a number of cases but clearly unacceptable in some others [since this situation de facto allows foreign entities to gather useful intelligence …]. In this respect, European military users are first and foremost affected by this issue of technological dependence and should primarily define their needs, concerns and objectives" (Tortora, 2015).

Ultimately, maintaining the status quo for Europe would mean remaining at the mercy of external forces and accepting a higher level of vulnerability with regard to both *security of supply* (unrestricted access to required technologies, products, services or information) and *supply chain security* (control of security throughout the programme lifecycle).

Conversely, becoming a space power would translate into greater industry and programmatic security, an objective that has been already acknowledged by the EU in its 2016 Space Strategy for Europe. Needless to say, such status would secure the many security payoffs already discussed in Sect. 2.3, including, most notably, a stronger projection of hard power on the international stage. These considerations are becoming exceedingly relevant in light of the unfolding geopolitical landscape worldwide—with increasing instability and turmoil around the European neighbourhood, the transition from a stable unipolar international system to a more turbulent multipolar world, global challenges related to climate and pollution, and the humanitarian implications of these developments.

Thus, there are key security stakes behind a possible pursuit of space power status. Nevertheless, one must acknowledge that security stakes might be not so persuasive for Europe as compared to other major powers. This is primarily due to the problematic nature of European integration, which has hindered any substantial advances in a pan-European military presence in space (or elsewhere). Although current developments in this field indicate a renewed interest and more optimistic perspective for a shared vision of European military space activities (such as the establishment of the European Defence Fund following the publication of a European Defence Action Plan, and the initiation of the PESCO framework), the overall outlook still greatly depends on broader political will towards Europe as a unified or even a single actor in the military domain per se.

4.2.1.3 Political Stakes

The major driver in fostering the position of Europe in the space power quadrant is anchored to this group of stakes. Indeed, from a political perspective, what is first and foremost at stake is European political sovereignty over the conduct of its space activities. Because getting critical technologies from non-European suppliers requires European stakeholders to obtain a green light from foreign authorities, it is clear that Europe faces significant political risks.

For one thing, it can be noted that Europe's lack of autonomy may impact its freedom of action and ultimately restrict its capability to decide when and under what conditions to develop and deploy its space programme. In addition, by maintaining the *status quo* Europe may not enjoy the autonomy to freely choose its partners, due to possible external pressures. The issue, however, is not limited to cooperation activities for highly sensitive projects such as Galileo. Civil and scientific cooperation may be also impacted, as already demonstrated by the case of past cooperation activities between India and France, for instance.

By the same token, the continued reliance on third party assets might deter third partners from proposing joint initiatives with Europe, because of Europe's need beforehand to secure a green light from foreign authorities, most notably the United States. All this may result in a sub-optimal implementation of policies and programmes that do not necessarily align with its interests. Therefore, by not pursuing the status of space power Europe will inevitably limit its freedom of action and political autonomy.

Equally important, dependence on the political will of external actors harms its prestige and bargaining power on the international stage, making European diplomatic efforts, its potential to influence others, and the exercise of soft power, less effective. This ultimately may preclude the continent from being a convincing agenda-setter within the international space community, a limitation that is already evident in those domains (such as for instance human spaceflight and space security) where Europe lacks the ability to rely on its own resources in the pursuit of declared objectives. Taking this into account, positioning Europe as a credible interlocutor in international dialogue and negotiations requires equipping the continent with independent capabilities to advance its interests.

Therefore, it makes political sense for Europe to realize and consequently develop its space power potential because, quote Nicolas Peter, what is "at stake is the future agenda-setting power of Europe in the international system, its ability to shape the priorities and timing of events, and its ability to attract the best partners to be able to fully benefit from opportunities wherever these support European space objectives and wider European policy goals" (Peter, 2009).

More broadly, what is at stake here is the long-term possibility for Europe to promote its position as a leader in space and strengthen its role as a global actor. This point has been already articulated by the EU in a number of policy documents, including the 2016 Space Strategy for Europe, which stressed that Europe's efforts to meet its strategic goals in the space arena will be undermined unless the EU achieves the broader goal of taking a much stronger role on the world stage. Achieving and maintaining the status of a space power means having the leverages to build its leadership in the global space sector at large.

4.2.2 A Matter of Political Will

Despite limited public demand for space-based services, little appetite for leadership competition, and intricate (space) governance, Europe has managed to position itself among the most prominent spacefaring actors worldwide, with a particular focus on the exploitation of space for socio-economic applications. Thanks to this focus and its emphasis on commercial markets and return on investment, Europe has been able "to quickly develop a fully-fledged competitive industry and to address the whole spectrum of space applications with just a fraction of the space budget of the United States, for instance" (Tortora, 2015).

More recently, Europe has started making its first steps in the realm of security and defence as a communitarian (space) actor, even though defence remains mostly structured in Europe at national level and, as of today, cannot be relied upon as a major driver behind European space efforts, unlike all other major space powers. By the same token, considerations of prestige have been certainly at work as a driver for several European endeavours (from the ISS to Rosetta), but they have not been very effective in stimulating public investments because of Europe's low appetite for international competition. In short, economic interests are still the key factor that will likely drive the European space agenda in the near future.

All these European specificities will influence, for better or the worse, the potential that Europe has as a spacefaring actor, and eventually a space power.

In fact, when linking the relevance of each of three groups of stakes to the above discussed specific policy drivers guiding past and current European space activities, a conundrum clearly emerges: European efforts in space are primarily driven by economic considerations. Yet economics is not the overarching stake associated with the pursuit of autonomy. In fact, the pursuit of autonomy (and consequently of space power status) proves to be first and foremost related to strategic (i.e. security and political) considerations (see Fig. 4.4).

Clearly, the decision to develop capacities—partially or along the full spectrum of capabilities, with a narrow or a wide scope—as well as the decision to do so with a high degree of autonomy or by relying on third countries' capabilities, is the result of a political process; a process that largely resembles the process that drives a country's decision to become a military power, or not. This means that any European decision in the direction of attaining space power status should be taken on purely political grounds.

From a political standpoint, achieving space power status is not only desirable, but also necessary, as what is at stake is Europe's political sovereignty over space matters and its declared objective to assert itself as a global player. However, even if

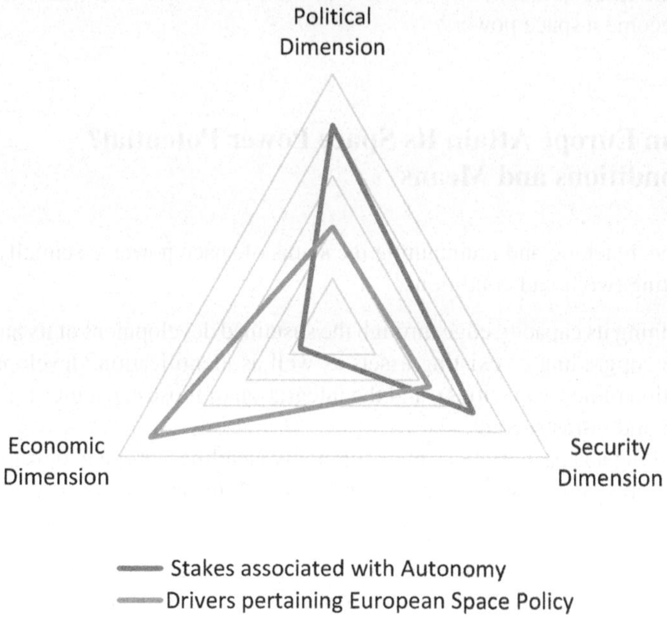

Fig. 4.4 Drivers and stakes: the European conundrum

the equation *no autonomy, no political sovereignty* provides a rather straightforward answer to the question of whether to aim at space power status, attaining such status is no easy undertaking. Quite to the contrary, the development and maintenance of such status is a capital-intensive process requiring not only sustained financial investments, but also the highest degree of political will and backing.

Political will is indeed the predominant precondition for a state to strive to attain space power, because as already put by Oberg:

> What, if anything, can we say that could qualify as a maxim in a state's drive to attain space power? Probably, only that: a state's drive to attain space power. When all layers are peeled away, what is left is a state's political will. In the absence of absolute wealth, as well as bureaucratic and technical inefficiencies, it was the political will of the Soviet Union to commit a disproportionate share of their national resources that enabled them to keep pace with the United States. It is also the policy in China, which views itself as the once and future "Middle Kingdom," where national will is responsible for an ascending space program in the midst of a myriad of competing national interests. And, most tellingly, it is the political backing of Israel's space program that has enabled that country to overcome the apparent obstacles to becoming a full-fledged member of the space community.
>
> Interestingly it is this very attribute—political will—that makes the European space endeavour so enigmatic. In combination, Europe has population, education, wealth, size, and suitable launch sites. And, it appears, only in combination does it have a future as a space power. However, it is questionable whether a combined political will can be found to drive the machinery of a space program comparable to that of the United States and the erstwhile Soviet Union. (Oberg, 1999, pp. 136, 137)

This dearth in political will is a highly critical and potentially fatal factor in tackling the issue of autonomy. In view of that, a new question, then, arises: *can* Europe become a space power?

4.3 Can Europe Attain Its Space Power Potential? Conditions and Means

For Europe, reaching and maintaining the status of space power essentially necessitates meeting two broad conditions:

- Maintaining its capacity edge through the sustained development of its hard capacities (i.e. upgrading of existing assets as well as identification, development and maturation of new capacities), and the integration of those capacities into national policies and infrastructure.
- Establishing an appropriate level of autonomy enabling Europe to develop and use its space programme without the necessity of seeking any kind of permission from anyone.

Each of these two conditions presents a number of cascading requirements, which are briefly detailed below. With respect to the time aspect, the short-term need is more apparent with respect to the issue of autonomy. From a long-term perspective, the requirements are related to both conditions.

4.3.1 *Maintaining High Capacities*

As identified in Sect. 3.2.3, Europe emerges from a capacity analysis with high scores—an achievement that should nonetheless not invite idleness or complacency. The ever-changing requirements associated with the status of space power as a consequence of technological progress create a need to maintain or even further improve Europe's capacity edge. Space technologies change, adapt and evolve, eventually allowing new types of space activities, new approaches to existing activities (cheaper, faster, more resilient …) and novel application and services opportunities to emerge. Europe must keep pace with global trends and potentially also be the trend-setter in specific areas of spaceflight. Philippe Brunet, then Director for Space Policy and Copernicus, DG GROW, recommended a course of action along the same lines at the High-Level Space Conference of the EU Council in November 2018. In his speech, Mr. Brunet advocated the pursuit of greater efficiency in all Europe's current activities and highlighted the need to invest in new promising concepts for Europe "to avoid waking up in ten years and realize that it has been left behind" (European Space Policy Institute, 2018, p. 20).

At this stage no conclusive assessment can be made of the extent to which currently emerging concepts such as reusability, in-orbit servicing, in-orbit manufacturing, or completely new concepts will impact the evolution of spacepower capabilities and the requirements to be met to attain space power status. However, it is clear that these requirements will evolve and broaden over time. This is an inevitable development of which European stakeholders need to be aware in order to act in a timely and appropriate manner.

Taking this into account, it is useful to visualize the trajectory of the capacity threshold in relation to Europe's position on the capacity matrix. Depending on how Europe's vision and efforts evolve, three broad scenarios can be envisioned, which are depicted in Fig. 4.5: one in which Europe maintains the current programmatic

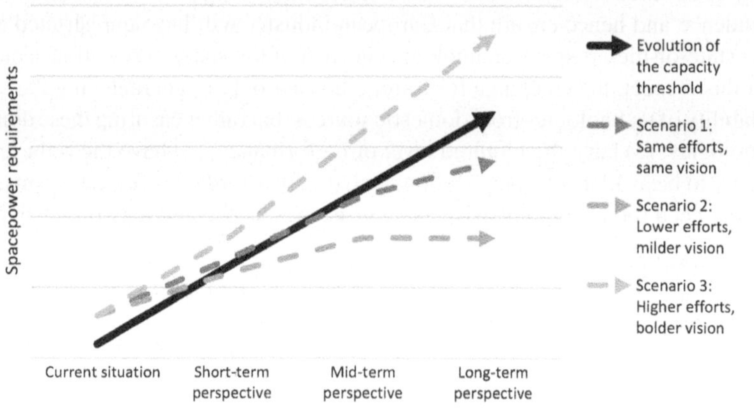

Fig. 4.5 Evolution of the requirements for the space power status, potential scenarios for Europe

profile, one scenario in which it reduces its space efforts, and one scenario in which it increases it efforts.

As the figure makes plain, in each of the three scenarios, Europe's position within the capacity matrix may not drastically change from a short-term perspective. However, only by adopting a bolder vision for its space programmes, and hence investing in the development of new capacities and making a further leap in integrating these capacities for the fulfilment of broader policy objectives, will Europe be able to remain above the capacity threshold over the medium to long term. In this context, it is certainly gratifying to see the proposal for the next MFF (2021–2027) that was approved by the European Parliament in December 2018, which endorsed a substantial increase of the initially proposed amount for the SSA and GOVSATCOM components of the EU Space Programme (EUR 1.2 billion compared to EUR 500 million in the original Commission proposal from June 2018[17]). As both SSA and secure governmental satellite communications are integral parts of the hard capacity and soft capacity indexes, the implementation of the two programmes will certainty contribute to maintaining Europe's high level of capacity.

However, beyond these well-defined programmes, new and more ground-breaking avenues must be explored if Europe is to maintain a leading position in the space pecking order and ensure that it will be the instigator rather than a victim of future technological developments.

4.3.2 Achieving Technological and Political Autonomy

The pursuit and maintenance of space power status in Europe is not only fraught with the burdensome issue of maintaining and enlarging its capacity edge, but also with the need to ensure that these capacities will be endowed with an appropriate level of autonomy over space matters. In attaining this objective, Europe will be primarily confronted with the need to tackle the longstanding problem of technological dependence and hence ensure that European industry will have unrestricted access to the state-of-the-art space technologies in each of the space application sectors.

In this respect, the challenge for Europe lies not only in guaranteeing the simple availability of technologies from domestic sources, but rather ensuring these domestic technologies: (a) have the required level of performance; (b) have the right level of maturity to be available for application; and, (c) are affordable. For these aims, there is a clear need for a comprehensive and consistent space technology policy that will:

[17]As of February 2019, negotiations on the final text (between the European Parliament, the Council of the European Union and the European Commission), and as such on specific budgetary allocations remained in progress. Procedurally, agreement on the final text of the regulation is needed from two legislative bodies—the European Parliament and the Council of the European Union.

- Address the different requirements in all application areas
- Support the complete value chain
- Foster adequate maturity and readiness.
- Target potential users.

While many initiatives and actions have been taken both within ESA and at EU level (finally converging in the Joint Task Force of the European Commission, ESA and EDA for European Technological Non-Dependence), an overall programmatic strategy at European level is still lacking (Caito, 2015).

In addition, it should be reiterated that European initiatives in the field have been focusing mostly on product concepts and the early stage of innovation, with a Technology Readiness Level (TRL) between 1 and 5. However, later phases of the technological process (high TRL) should also be properly covered to ensure the ultimate availability of these technologies and relieve the users from the financial burdens and risks associated with the full qualification of the required technologies. In this respect, qualification and in-orbit validation are essential steps to bring innovative technologies to the right level for risk-free implementation in European programmes and for commercialisation. Therefore, more attention should be given to the maturity and readiness aspects. This is a challenging task, since it requires harmonisation of potentially conflicting priorities as well as an institutionally-funded mechanism that can completely bring European technologies within an application or operational programme.

It is worth highlighting that the issue of maturation of technologies was seriously addressed in the U.S. with the creation of Defense Advanced Research Projects Agency (DARPA) in 1958. To date no equivalent structure can be found in Europe. Interestingly, the argument underpinning the need for a "European DARPA" was recently brought under the spotlight by the European Commission at the European Space Policy Conference in January 2019. On that occasion, the EU Commissioner Elżbieta Bieńkowska hinted at the establishment of a European Innovation Council (EIC), with space technologies being at the core of such an innovation effort. Whereas it cannot be anticipated whether such an initiative will prove appropriate given its current status,[18] one such development underscores that Europe's need to identify effective solutions for carrying out the complete qualification of new technologies and limit cost overruns of European space programmes is well understood.

In addition to technology maturation, measures to support the eventual commercialisation of the matured technologies should also be provided. It is evident that "it would make no sense to publicly fund the complete development cycle of a new

[18] With a cumulative budget of EUR 13 billion in the period 2019–2027, it claims that the overarching purpose of the EIC is to bring ground-breaking new technologies to market. Even though the maturation of technologies has not been explicitly introduced in this regard, the EIC pilot project (2018–2020) aims to finance innovation activities such as demonstration, testing, piloting and scaling up. Providing continuity between the current and next MFF (2021–2027), it is anticipated that full-fledged EIC will be tackling higher technology readiness levels, which falls in line with argumentation provided in this study. What remains to seen is its ultimate effectiveness in practice.

technology for pure non-dependence purposes if nothing is done to ensure that it will actually be used as an alternative to non-European sources eventually available" (Tortora, 2015, p. 170). Addressing this demanding issue will require either to (a) enact adapted procurement rules to implement long-term agreements with European suppliers, or (b) provide sustained support for the competitiveness of the European industry.

Clearly, all these activities require a sustained financial effort on the public side, the establishment of sound industrial processes/production facilities, and an authoritative institutional setting tasked with their operational implementation. While substantial, the effort is arguably within the realm of Europe's potential, provided there is a strong commitment on the political side.[19] The question, once again, becomes whether European stakeholders are prepared and willing to pay the price for their autonomy.

In offering a conclusive answer to this question, it must first be acknowledged that commitment is present among all the major pan-European institutions (ESA, the European Commission and EDA). However, in light of the governance framework discussed above, determining the operational body responsible for the implementation of these activities is a decision to be taken at the political level by member states. In fact, at this stage none of the European institutional actors would be fully equipped to effectively deal with the issue in a sustained manner without a concerted agreement among European countries.

Member States do not equally share concerns over the issue of autonomy—and ultimately European sovereignty. This clearly undermines the efficiency with which Europe can tackle the issue of technological dependence. Furthermore, it once again demonstrates how the political dependencies embedded in the current setting generate restrictions that ultimately preclude Europe from moving beyond the status of a "spacefaring region".

Because "Europe's many voices and often conflicting national interests significantly weaken its ability to act in a cohesive let alone sustained manner" (Schubert, 2015), Europe must find ways to offset or overcome these restrictions and its lack of an autonomous profile on the political level if it is to assert itself as a space power. This implies finding ways to mend the fragmented landscape and skilfully craft an effective one-voice system capable of forging a common strategic vision for space matters. Incidentally, one proposal along these lines was recently made by European Commissioner Bieńkowska on the establishment of a European Space Council:

> In the U.S. they have a National Space Council attached directly to the President. Why couldn't we have a European Space Council attached directly to the European Council or its President? It would gather all the space decision makers and actors, and advise directly our heads of states and government. (European Commission, 2019)

The logic behind the proposal is simple and compelling: by shifting the venue of discussions on Europe's direction and strategic ambition in space from the current

[19] According to Eurospace, an effort in the order of few hundred million per year would suffice to tackle the issue of non-dependence.

ministerial level[20] to the highest political level, a much-needed alignment of views among European heads of states and government and consequently a shared long-term vision for Europe in space could be reached. The proposed Council could thus mend the fragmented landscape and be entrusted with the mission of drafting a longstanding common strategy for Europe "on crucial issues such as strategic autonomy, economic and industrial policy, space security and defence, diplomacy or, in general, any topic that needs to be addressed at the highest political level to stimulate decision-making processes and ensure consistency of action" (European Space Policy Institute, 2019).

This may prove an important stepping-stone towards emphasising the comprehensive strategic nature of the European space sector and, more importantly, filling Europe's autonomy gap in the political realm. It is also clear, however, that to achieve full political autonomy and attain its space power potential, a more ambitious political evolution of the overall institutional setting will be ultimately indispensable.

To echo the admonition of the EU High Representative, Europe's goal to become a space power can only be achieved as a truly united and committed Europe. As long as European member states do not jointly see the need to move beyond the current intergovernmental model and confer real autonomy over space matters to the supranational level, the possibility for Europe to become a full-fledged space power will inexorably remain untapped.

References

Algieri, F. (2015). In search of shared autonomy: The EU as a restricted foreign, security and defence political actor. In C. Al-Ekabi (Ed.), *European autonomy in space* (pp. 93–104). Vienna: Springer.

Aliberti, M. (2015). *When China goes to the moon...*. Vienna: Springer.

Aliberti, M., & Lahcen, A. (2015). *The future of European flagship programmes in space*. Vienna: European Space Policy Institute.

Aliberti, M., & Lisitsyna, K. (2019). *Russia's posture in space—Prospects for europe*. Vienna: Springer.

Aliberti, M., Sarret, M., Hrozensky, T., Perrichon, L., & Rowley, J. (2018). *Security in outer space: Transatlantic relations*. Vienna: European Space Policy Institute.

Bordacchini, G., & Burger, E. (2018). *Space policies, issues and trends in 2017–2018*. Vienna: European Space Policy Institute.

Caito, L. (2015). *European technological non-dependence in space*. Vienna: European Space Policy Institute.

Copernicus Security Service. (n.d.). Retrieved February 16, 2019, from Copernicus: https://www.copernicus.eu/en/services/security.

[20]The two main bodies providing policy guidelines on a short to medium-term and characterizing the drivers for action of ESA and the EU are organized at ministerial level. These are the ESA Ministerial Councils, which every two or three years gather all ministers responsible for space affairs to decide about new programmatic proposals and funding, and the EC's Competitiveness Council (COMPET), which depending on the national distribution of space competencies, convenes ministers responsible for trade, economy, industry, transport, or research and innovation to discuss relevant agenda items on a case-by-case basis.

Draghi, M. (2019, February 22). *Sovereignty in a globalised world.* Retrieved from European Central Bank: https://www.ecb.europa.eu/press/key/date/2019/html/ecb.sp190222~fc5501c1b1.en.html.

European Commission. (2017). *Technologies for European non-dependence and competitiveness (critical space technologies)—Guidance document for Horizon 2020 work programme 2018–2020.* Brussels: European Commission.

European Commission. (2018a). *Horizon 2020—Work programme 2018–2020, leadership in enabling and industrial technologies—Space.* European Commission.

European Commission. (2018b). *Proposal for a regulation of the European Parliament and of the Council establishing the space programme of the Union and the European Union Agency for the space programme.* Brussels: European Commission.

European Commission. (2018c). *Report from the Commission to the European Parliament and the Council on the implementation of the Space Surveillance and Tracking (SST) support framework (2014–2017).* Brussels: European Commission.

European Commission. (2018d). *Technologies for European non-dependence and competitiveness—Guidance document for Horizon 2020 work programme 2018–2020.* European Commission.

European Commission. (2019, January 22). *11th annual conference on European space policy—Opening speech.* Retrieved February 16, 2019, from European Commission: https://ec.europa.eu/commission/commissioners/2014-2019/bienkowska/announcements/11th-annual-conference-european-space-policy-opening-speech_en.

European Space Agency, European Commission. (2017). *European space technology master plan.*

European Space Policy Institute. (2017). *Europe: Out of the box.* Vienna: European Space Policy Institute.

European Space Policy Institute. (2018). *High-level space conference of the EU Council "#EUSpace for Business"—Outcome report.* Vienna: European Space Policy Institute.

European Space Policy Institute. (2019). *Perspective on a European Space Council.* Vienna: European Space Policy Institute.

Eurospace. (2018). *Facts and figures press release—14th June 2018: The state of the European space industry in 2017.* Eurospace.

Federal Communications Commission. (2018). *FCC FACT SHEET—Receive-only earth stations operating with the Galileo radionavigation-satellite service.* Washington, DC: Federal Communications Commission.

Fonseca, A. (2013). *ESA cooperation with Russia, China, Brazil, India and South Africa.* Leiden: European Space Agency.

Galileo Security Monitoring Centre. (2016, June 20). Retrieved February 16, 2019, from European GNSS Agency: https://www.gsa.europa.eu/security/gsmc.

Gilmore, R. (2012, November 06). Retrieved from European Space Components Information Exchange System: https://escies.org/download/webDocumentFile?id=49190.

Hill, C., & Smith, M. (2005). *International relations and the European Union.* Oxford: Oxford University Press.

Kissinger, H. (2014). *World order.* New York: Penguin Press.

Krasner, S. D. (1999). *Sovereignty: Organized hipocrisy.* Princeton, NJ: Princeton University Press.

Mineiro, M. C. (2011). An inconvenient regulatory truth: Divergence in US and EU satellite export control policies on China. *Space Policy, 27*(2), 213–221.

Moranta, S., Pavesi, G., Perrichon, L., Plattard, S., & Sarret, M. (2018). *Security in outer space: Rising stakes for Europe.* Vienna: European Space Policy Institute.

Oberg, J. E. (1999). *Space power theory.* Colorado Springs: U.S. Air Force Academy.

Peter, N. (2009). *Space power and Europe in the 21st century.* Vienna: European Space Policy Institute.

PwC. (2016). *Socio-economic impacts from space activities in the EU in 2015 and beyond.* European Union.

PwC. (2017). *Dependence of the European economy on space infrastructures—Potential impacts of space assets loss.* European Union.

Robinson, J. (2011). *Enabling Europe's key foreign policy objectives via space*. Vienna: European Space Policy Institute.

Schubert, S. R. (2015). Lessons for European autonomy in space from past pursuit of energy autonomy. In C. Al-Ekabi (Ed.), *European autonomy in space* (pp. 77–91). Vienna: Springer.

Tortora, J.-J. (2015). European autonomy in space: The technological dependence. In C. Al-Ekabi (Ed.), *European autonomy in space* (pp. 165–172). Vienna: Springer.

Wallace, W. (2005). Post-sovereign governance: The EU as a partial polity. In H. Wallace, W. Wallace, & M. A. Pollack (Eds.), *Policy-making in the European Union* (pp. 483–503). Oxford: Oxford University Press.

Zhao, Y., & Bian, Y. (2011). Export control regime for space items in China: Opportunities and challenges in the new era. *Space Policy, 27*(2), 107–112.

Chapter 5
Concluding Remarks

This study has made a comparative assessment of the major space actors worldwide. The underlying objective was to examine Europe's relative position in space and put into perspective its purported ambition to assert itself as a *space power* with the necessary means and resources required to meet this goal.

Towards this, the study first integrated and ordered the academic debate by methodically defining and explaining the concepts of *spacepower* and *space power*. Building on this, the study focused on the creation of a new theoretical framework to empirically compare various space actors on the basis of measurable criteria and indicators. More specifically, starting from a status-based definition of space power (i.e. an entity with the means to autonomously deploy, operate and benefit from any space-related capability to support the achievement of national objectives), the study identified the underlying conditions for attaining such status.

In order to assess the extent to which these conditions are present in different countries, a set of four indexes encompassing a total of 68 entries have been developed. As graphically summarised in Fig. 5.1, capacity has been evaluated on the basis of the *hard* and *soft* capacity indexes, while autonomy has been measured on the basis of the *technical* and *political* autonomy indexes.

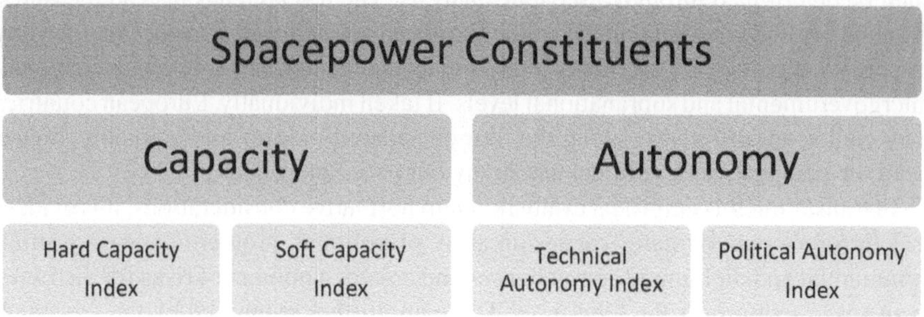

Fig. 5.1 Breakdown of space power constituents

M. Aliberti et al., *Measuring Space Power*,
SpringerBriefs from the European Space Policy Institute,
https://doi.org/10.1007/978-3-030-15754-8_5

The heuristic utility of these four indexes (hard and soft capacity indexes, and technological and political autonomy indexes) is that they delineate and characterise different typologies of space actors and provide key tools to identify, measure and compare their strengths and weaknesses. It is also clear, however, that the elements identified as part of the capacity and autonomy indexes are neither exhaustive nor seamless. It is therefore possible—and even recommendable—that future studies integrate the indexes with other elements. Equally important, additional steps should be taken to further refine the evaluation criteria used to obtain the capacity and autonomy indexes, set the relative thresholds, and handle comparative assessments among the selected countries in a more detailed manner. Due to issues with data availability and comparability, several indicators were assessed through a qualitative approach, but it is clear that a quantitative approach should be preferred to ensure more uniform and reproducible assessments and avoid normative biases, especially when it comes to empirically politically-loaded indicators, such as the degree of autonomy of an actor.

From the empirical application of the theoretical framework to the *Big Six in Space*, it emerged that the U.S., China and Russia, can be considered as space powers, being all endowed with high capacity and high autonomy. With considerable autonomy but somewhat less capacity, Japan and India qualifies as "rising space nations" that nearly meet the capacity criteria of a full-fledged space power.

Conversely, Europe emerges from the analysis as a powerful "spacefaring region". This is the by-product of the imbalance between Europe's high level of capacity (in both the hard and soft dimensions), and a relatively low level of autonomy in the technological and political spheres. While Europe can boast significant achievements in its space endeavours and is equipped with a highly capable and competitive industry in a broad range of space domains, it does not, as yet, possess technological autonomy across the full spectrum of space capabilities and, more importantly, has only a limited degree of political autonomy over space matters. As discussed in the study, the political dependencies embedded in the current setting are a specific feature of the European polity.

It is important to reiterate in this context that the results of this empirical assessment are not applicable to individual European countries, the current status of which shall be determined through a separate analysis. The research has instead measured the capacity and autonomy levels of the European space programme per se, focusing on specific qualities of "actorness" that stem from the interplay between the national, intergovernmental and supranational levels. If taken individually, European countries may well score differently along the four considered indexes and, arguably, higher from the perspective of political autonomy but lower on capacity.

In translating this empirical evaluation into normative considerations, it is evident that Europe's current status carries an array of political, programmatic, industrial, commercial and diplomatic consequences and creates a number of risks for the European space sector over the long-term. These are further magnified by the mismatch between Europe's declared ambitions and the actual means to achieve them. This mismatch hence calls for a revisiting of the overarching policy drivers of the European approach to space towards a more politically-oriented profile, if Europe is to assert itself as a full-fledged space power.

In this context, the study examined the strategic stakes associated with such status and clarified the motives underpinning its possible pursuit. At the same time, it also highlighted the many issues that would come with the quest for such status. These include: the need to put in place effective instruments to tackle the issue of technological dependence; the necessity of revisiting the concept of shared competency in space affairs; the need for a more ambitious agenda in the foreign, security and defence policy; and the need to address the reluctance of Member States to agree on any additional transfer of sovereignty towards European institutions in this area.

Given these burdensome issues that must be overcome, it is clear that Europe's path towards space power status will be a lengthy process ultimately demanding a deeper advancement of the political dimension of the European integration project. Recovering unity of vision and action will be the key tool to fully attain Europe's space power potential. Eventually, Europe *can* be and *should* be a space power. But if wants to achieve this goal effectively, it must first push forward the construction of Europe.

Annex

List of Definitions of Spacepower and Space Power

1988—Lupton, On Space Warfare
[…] spacepower is the ability of a nation to exploit the space environment in pursuit of national goals and purposes and includes the entire astronautical capabilities of the nation. A nation with such capabilities is termed a space power (Lupton, 1988, p. 4).
1994—Larned @ Air and Space Doctrine Symposium
Spacepower is the ability to exploit the civil, commercial and national security space systems and associated infrastructure in support of national security strategy (Jusell, 1998, p. 8).
1995—Hyatt, Space Power 2010
Space power is the ability of a state or non-state actor to achieve its goals and objectives in the presence of other actors on the world stage through control and exploitation of the space environment (Hyatt, Paul, Rampino, Ricchi, & Schwarz, 1995, p. 5).
1996—Gray, The influence of Space Power upon History
Space power may be defined as the ability to use space while denying reliable use to any foe (Gray, 1996, p. 293).

Space power, as mentioned above, refers simply to the ability to use space for military, civil, or commercial purposes and to deny the ability of an enemy to do the same. This functional, output oriented definition (tightly linked to the ability of the nation to control vital spaceways) is preferable to a strictly unilateral, descriptive usage and parallels common definitions of air power and sea power. Any concept which embraces the word "power" accepts the ambiguities of that difficult term (Gray, 1996, p. 299).
1998—Air Force Doctrine Document 2-2, Space Operations
In text: Space power is the capability to employ space forces to achieve national security objectives (U.S. Air Force, 1998, p. 1).

M. Aliberti et al., *Measuring Space Power*,
SpringerBriefs from the European Space Policy Institute
https://doi.org/10.1007/978-3-030-15754-8

Glossary: [Space Power:] The capability to exploit civil, commercial, intelligence, and national security space systems and associated infrastructure to support national security strategy and national objectives from peacetime through combat operations (U.S. Air Force, 1998, p. 32).

1998—Scott Pace et al., Space: Emerging Options for National Power

Spacepower is connected to other forms of national power such as economic strength, scientific capabilities, and international leadership. [...] Therefore, we would define spacepower as *the pursuit of national objectives through the medium of space and the use of space capabilities.* [...] The effective exercise of spacepower may require, but it is not limited to, the use of military force (Johnson, Pace, & Gabbard, 1998, p. 8).

1999—Oberg, Space Power Theory

Space power is the combination of technology, demographic, economic, industrial, military, national will, and other factors that contribute to the coercive and persuasive ability of a country to politically influence the actions of other states and other kinds of players, or to otherwise achieve national goals through space activity (Oberg, 1999, p. 10).

1999—Gray et al., Space Power and the Revolution in Military Affairs: A Glass Half Full?

If space power is defined as the ability in peace, crisis, and war to exert prompt and sustained influence in or from space then the key enabler for space power has to be space control (Gray & Sheldon, 1999, p. 36).

2001—Logsdon, Just Say Wait to Space Power

Space power can be defined as using the space medium and assets located in space to enhance and project U.S. military power (Logsdon, 2001).

2002—Joint Publication 3-14, Space Operations

The total strength of a nation's capabilities to conduct and influence activities to, in, through, and from space to achieve its objectives (Joint Chiefs of Staff, 2002, p. GL-6).

2006—Harter, Ten Propositions Regarding Space Power—The Dawn of a Space Force

Space power—a nation's ability to exploit and control the space medium to support and achieve national goals (Harter, 2006, p. 67).

2008—Lutes, Spacepower in the 21st Century

Spacepower, then, might be defined as the ability to use space to influence other actors and the external environment to achieve one's objectives. Spacepower both contributes to and is supported by other forms of power: diplomatic, informational, military, and economic, among others. Spacepower can be looked at through sociocultural, economic, and security lenses, each roughly equating to the civil-scientific, commercial, and military intelligence sectors of space activity (Lutes, 2008, p. 67).

2008—Peter, Space Power and Europe

Space power can be defined as the "total strength and ability of a State to conduct and influence activities to, in, through and from space to achieve its goals and objectives (security, economic and political), to affect desired outcomes in the presence of other actors in the world stage and if necessary to change the behaviour of others by exploiting the space systems and associated ground-infrastructure as well as political leverage it has garnered" (Peter, 2009).

2011—Toward a Theory of Spacepower: Selected Essays

Our working definition of spacepower is the sum total of capabilities that contribute to a nation's ability to benefit from the use of space (Kepron, Hitchens, & Katz-Hyman, 2011, p. 391).

2012—Al-Rodhan, Meta-Geopolitics of Outer Space

I define *space power* as the ability of a state to use space to sustain and enhance its seven state capacities as outlined in the meta-geopolitics framework, namely (social and health, domestic politics, economics, environment, science and human potential, military and security, and international diplomacy). In addition, the governance and sustainability of space power will need to employ a "symbiotic realism" approach to global relations and a "multi-sum security principle" approach to global security. Ultimately, space will either be safe for everyone or for no one (Al-Rodhan, 2012, p. 25).

List of Spacepower Theories

Year	Author	Work	Content
1988	Lupton	On Space Warfare	Identifies four potential space power doctrines—the sanctuary doctrine, the survivability doctrine, the high-ground doctrine, the control doctrine—with the Control Doctrine being considered the best to employ space forces
1995	Hyatt, et al.	Space Power 2010	The authors define military space power, six concepts of operations (CONOPS)—space strike, information blockade, space denial, omniscience/omnipresence, operational spacelift, and massively proliferated and networked microsat constellations—and the requirements to implement such operations
1995	Mantz	The New Sword: A Theory of Space Combat Power	The author develops a list of axioms of space combat power, focusing on "space strike systems", "space denial systems", space protection, and space control, calling for a centralized control of space combat power, and emphasizing that spacepower is not intrinsically linked to airpower
1996	Gray	The Influence of Space Power Upon History	Starting from warfare, airpower and seapower considerations, the author emphasizes the need for a Mahan theorist for space, as a "Mahanian

(continued)

(continued)

Year	Author	Work	Content
			analysis of the elements of, and conditions for, space power has yet to be undertaken"
1998	Jusell	Space Power Theory: A Rising Star	Comparing current space power theories, the author suggests the need for a single comprehensive theory, identifying two critical issues to be addressed: space control and space force organization
1999	Oberg	Space Power Theory	Starting from classical theorists, Oberg lists the elements contributing to spacepower—facilities, technology, industry, hardware and other products, economy, populace, education, tradition and intellectual climate, visionary leadership, geography, and exclusivity of capabilities and knowledge. He then lists truths and beliefs on which can be based space power theories for the near-term, as long-term encompassing theories are limited by the current (1999) level of technological development for space
2000	France	Back to the Future: Space Power Theory and A. T. Mahan	The author comparers seapower, as defined by Mahan, with spacepower, looking at the differences emerging between Mahan's sea control strategies and today's approaches to space control, suggesting that spacefaring nations should draw more lessons from the naval theorist
2001	Dolman	Astropolitik	Starting by outlining geopolitical theories, with a particular consideration for Mackinder's Heartland theory, the author envisions a realpolitik-inspired framework for space, suggesting a three-step plan for a country—the U. S. in the author's mind—to dominate earth and near-earth space
2001	Fox	Some Principles of Space Strategy	The author compares Mahan's seapower theory to Corbet's maritime theory and how the latter is more apt to describe the relationship between spacepower and other forms of military powers, drawing strategic lessons from the comparison of the Corbettian concept of sea control with space control

(continued)

(continued)

Year	Author	Work	Content
2001	Smith	Ten Propositions Regarding Spacepower	Building from Lupton's doctrines, and affirming that air and space are different warfare dominions, the author lists ten propositions "to help train the judgments of political and military practitioners". These are: space is a distinct operational medium; the essence of spacepower is global access and global presence; spacepower is composed of a state's total space activity; spacepower must be centrally controlled by a space professional; spacepower is a coercive force; commercial space assets make all actors space powers; spacepower assets form a national centre of gravity; space control is not optional; space professionals require career-long specialization; weaponizing space is inevitable
2005	Wagner	Spacepower Theory: Lessons From the masters	Comparing the thought of classical theorists of land, sea, and airpower, the author draws five lessons for a space power theory: Spacepower must control space lines of communication; decisive points are key to space control; spacepower requires superior observation capabilities and the ability to take offensive action; robust spacepower could lead to enemy paralysis; and spacepower requires masters (classical theorists) of the space medium
2006	Fredriksson	Globalness: Toward a Space Power Theory	The author aims to contribute to the creation of a military space power theory, given the necessity of having a theory as space power is a separate and unique form of military power, and not only a force multiplier. The "globalness" of space is thus considered the unifying principle for a list of laws and rules of space power
2006	Harter	Ten Propositions Regarding Space Power	The author elaborates ten propositions on space power and five propositions on space characteristics—space is the ultimate high-ground; space is a distinct medium; space

(continued)

(continued)

Year	Author	Work	Content
			power is a force multiplier for every combatant commander and military service; space forces can support all levels of war, simultaneously space power leverages a nations economic and military centres of gravity—as well as five propositions on space challenges—space superiority starts with assured access to space; controlling space requires eyes, ears, shields and swords; space forces require centralized command and control led by space professionals; space power is a function of a nation's total space capability; national space power reaches its full potential when a nation commits to a separate, independent space force
2006	Klein	Space Warfare	Based on Corbett's Maritime strategic principles, the author builds a framework of strategic principles of space warfare, being able to use such framework to provide policy recommendations such as, for instance, on arms control regulations
2009	Havercroft, Duvall	Critical Geopolitics	Analysing space power theories through the lenses of realism and liberal-republicanism, the authors comment on a Dolman-inspired Astropolitik scenario, arguing that, in contrast to Dolman's conclusions, a space-based empire would hardly be a benevolent one
2011	Lutes, Hays, et al.	Towards a Theory of Spacepower: Selected Essays	A selection of essays covering multiple aspects of spacepower theories. Many insights are provided by considering classical power theorists and more recent spacepower theorists, in addition to original contributions
2011	Swilley	Space Power: A Theory for Sustaining U.S. Security Through the Information Age	The author highlights the links between space power theories and national interests, analysing the concept of great power status, providing an overview on current space power theories, and eventually supporting those theorists who translated Mahanian principles from seapower to spacepower

(continued)

(continued)

Year	Author	Work	Content
2014	Hays, et al.	Spacepower Theory	The author compares existing spacepower theories, considering Dolman and Oberg among the theorists worth mentioning, listing potential challenges that need to be addressed by a spacepower theory for the future, including sustainability, in-orbit wealth production, planetary defence

Matrix Evaluation Elements

As introduced in Chap. 2, the capacity and autonomy indexes have been subdivided in areas, each encompassing a number of entries. In order to evaluate these entries with the scoring system described in Chap. 3, both quantitative data sets and qualitative evaluations have been utilised. In the following tables, the elements considered to evaluate the entries are detailed. Quantitative assessments are marked in green, qualitative ones in blue. Quantitative evaluations have been primarily based on the statistics from the Space Activity Database of the European Space Policy Institute (ESPI). Qualitative evaluations are the result of the work of a dedicated focus group of six ESPI researchers, each possessing a geographical/sectorial expertise relevant to the conduct of the comparative assessment. Entries' descriptions are not exhaustive and are intended only as a reference point of the interpretive analysis conducted at ESPI.[1]

Hard Capacity Index

The elements have been considered to evaluate hard capacity are all based on quantitative data, here listed in the third column of the table.

[1]The ESPI database is a repository of information on global space activity, including launch events (date, launch site, outcome, launcher, spacecraft and service provider); worldwide spacecraft information (customer, orbit, mass, manufacturer, payloads, mission and market), etc. The database architecture allows the user to create dedicated field and categories to tailor specific analysis. Besides ESPI internal database and publications, additional sources consulted to evaluate entries include the works and publications of the following institutions: ASD-Eurospace, the Organisation for Economic Co-operation and Development (OECD), the Japanese Center for Research and Development Strategy, the Space Foundation, Secure World Foundation, PriceWaterhouseCooper (PwC), and Satsearch.

Areas	Entries	Elements considered	
Access to space	Number of launches	The number of successful launches, including launches that partially failed, albeit leaving the spacecraft in a useful orbit and operational	
	Launchers variety	Diversity of launchers available in the period considered, including launchers no longer available today	
	Performance	The current maximum payload that the largest national launcher can position in GTO, considering current operational launchers	
	Reliability	The ratio between successful launches over total launches in the considered period, not considering demo flights	
	Flexibility	Compatibility between major launchers and payloads by major manufacturers	
Ground segment	Ground stations	Series of indicators listing capacity of national deep space networks, availability of mobile receiving stations as ships, commercial diffusion of ground stations	
	Launch facilities	Quantity and variety of launch pads in terms of number and latitudes	
	Integration and test facilities	Presence and number of integration and test facilities in the national territory	
	Mission control centres	Presence and relevance (in terms of mission capacity) of mission control centres	
Operational space systems	(Remote sensing) Number of satellites	Number of remote sensing satellites launched in the period considered	
	(Remote sensing) Variety of sensor types	Variety of remote sensing sensors aboard satellites launched in the considered period	
	(Remote sensing) Variety of performance	Variety of performance offered by remote sensors aboard satellites launched in the considered period	
	(Remote sensing) Mission diversity	Variety of satellites' purposes, considering earth observation, early warning, meteorology, SSA, signal intelligence	
	(Navigation) Performance	Assessment of technologies contributing to the system architecture: SIS-URE index, on-board atomic clocks precision	
	(Navigation) Coverage	Coverage of the navigation satellite system (regional, global, under deployment)	
	(Navigation) Augmentation	Comparison of features, coverage and status (under development, under deployment, fully operational) of SBAS systems	
	(Communications) Number of satellites	Number of telecom-related satellites launched in the period considered	
	(Communications) Technological prowess	Technological complexity of nationally built/operated satellites	
	(Communications) Mission diversity	Variety of satellites' purposes, dividing the purpose into telecom, AIS, data relay	
Science and exploration	Number of missions	Number of missions launched in the considered period	
	Space science	Astronomical and fundamental research via space missions, number and complexity of missions	

	Earth science	Number of earth science satellites launched in the considered period	
	Diversity of destination	Diversity of locations targeted in the solar system, with a bonus for exotic locations never visited by others	
	Spacecraft variety	Diversity of the mission nature, considering rovers, landers, orbiters, probes, sample returns	
	Number of operational missions	Number of currently operational missions that escaped earth orbit	
Human spaceflight	Astronauts	Number of national astronauts and training facilities on national territory	
	Cargo capsules	Available proven technology: expertise but not hardware, hardware (not retrievable, no station boost capabilities), frequent use of hardware (retrievable, and or with station boost capabilities)	
	Crew capsules	Available proven technology: expertise but no hardware or announced development, active development/close to flight, current utilization	
	Infrastructures and modules	Level of contribution to space stations missions, considering components, single modules, full-fledged space stations	
	EVAs	Amount of experience with EVAs, amount of cumulated time spent spacewalking	
	Human-rated launcher	Available proven technology: expertise but no hardware or announced development, active development/close to flight, current utilization	
SSA and counter-space	Space surveillance and tracking	Extent of development of SST assets and capabilities	
	Space weather and NEOs	Number of missions to monitor NEOs and NEOs discovered; provision of operational SWE services for critical infrastructure protection	
	Maturity of counter-space capabilities	Maturity of direct ascent technology, co-orbital-related technology, direct energy-related technology, cyber warfare capabilities and electronic warfare capabilities	
	Variety of counter-space capabilities	Variety of counter-space assets (direct ascent technology, co-orbital-related technology, direct energy-related technology, cyber warfare capabilities and electronic warfare capabilities)	

Soft capacity Index

Given the complexity and span of soft capacities in integrating and utilizing space for national policies, and in particular for matters related to socio-economic policies, soft capacities have been evaluated mostly qualitatively. The evaluation is the result on the work of dedicated focus group at ESPI.

Areas	Entries	Elements considered	
Socio-economic policies	Natural resources	Integration of satellite applications in the agriculture industry	
		Integration of satellite applications in the forestry industry	
		Integration of satellite applications in the fishing industry	
		Integration of satellite applications in the mining industry	
	Energy production and distribution	Integration of satellite applications in site identification and monitoring	
		Integration of satellite applications in infrastructure monitoring	
		Integration of satellite applications in pipelines and grids timing and synchronization	
		Integration of satellite applications in communications networks	
	Meteorology and environment	Integration of satellite applications in weather forecasting	
		Integration of satellite applications in water resources monitoring	
		Integration of satellite applications in climate change monitoring	
		Integration of satellite applications in biodiversity and ecosystem protection	
	Infrastructure development	Integration of satellite applications in the construction industry	
		Integration of satellite applications in the logistics industry	
		Integration of satellite applications in the management of telecom networks	
		Integration of satellite applications in the financial sector	
	Transport and mobility	Integration of satellite applications for land, water, air navigation	
		Integration of satellite applications in fleet management systems	
		Integration of satellite applications for maps and charts	
		Integration of satellite applications in land, water, air traffic monitoring and management	
		Integration of satellite applications for vehicles, vessels, and planes tracking and/or identification	
		Integration of satellite applications for goods tracking	
		Integration of satellite applications for alarm systems, eCall, etc.	
		Integration of satellite applications in search and rescue related devices	
		Integration of satellite applications to enhance telecom capabilities (via train and in remote areas, at sea, air, inflight connectivity, etc.)	

	Rural and urban development	Integration of satellite applications in drinking water management	
		Integration of satellite applications in wasteland management	
		Integration of satellite applications in watershed development and monitoring	
		Integration of satellite applications for telecoms	
		Integration of satellite applications in surveying and mapping	
		Integration of satellite applications in the management of master and structure plan of cities	
		Integration of satellite applications in urban sprawl mapping	
		Integration of satellite applications for the development plans of town/cities	
	Health, education and lifestyle	Integration of satellite applications in entertainment, commercial broadcasting	
		Integration of satellite applications for remote learning and educational programmes	
		Integration of satellite applications for telemedicine	
		Open data services and policies related to national satellite-based information	
	Market development	Commercial revenues in upstream and downstream segments	
		Number of private actors	
		Number of spinoffs	
Foreign policies	Utilization of space for diplomatic purposes	Extent to which space is used for political gains	
		Extent to which space is used for strategic gains	
		Extent to which space is used for material gains (e.g. economic returns)	
	Creation of soft power narrative	Extent to which space as a national tradition is used to foster national pride	
		Extent to which space is used to earn/reinforce national prestige	
		Extent to which space is used for outreach	
		Extent to which national space programmes are perceived as reliable by foreigners	
	Active participation in international decision-making process	Participation in selected organizations	
		Membership to selected treaties	
		Number of cooperation agreements/partnerships	
		Presence of capacity sharing schemes	
Security and defence	Integration of space in national security policies	Utilisation of space data to support to policy making	
		Extent to which space is used to implement infrastructure security	
		Presence of space (assets) security legislation and strategies	
		Extent to which space is considered within the realm of national cybersecurity strategies and policies	

	Use of space for surveillance, verification and risk assessment	Extent to which space is used to enhance domestic security (border and maritime surveillance, infrastructure protection, etc.)	
		Extent to which space is used for international security purposes (treaty verification, countering proliferation of WMD, etc.)	
	Use of space in crisis and disaster management	Extent to which space is used within warning systems	
		Extent to which space is used for damage assessment	
		Extent to which space is used for search and rescue operations	
		Extent to which space is used for relief and recovery operations	
	Integration of space in national military strategy	Extent to which space is used for prevention and deterrence of hostile actions	
		Extent to which space is used to pursue control of the land, sea, air and space medium	
		Extent to which space is integrated in ballistic missile defence	
	Use of space in military operations	Extent to which space is integrated within Command, Control, Communications, Computing (C4)	
		Extent to which space is used for military intelligence, surveillance and reconnaissance capabilities (ISR), including early warning, signal interception and active observation	
		Extent to which PNT-based applications (missile guidance, UAV piloting, etc.) are used	
		Extent to which space is integrated in other military support services (augmentation of terrestrial technologies such as weather forecasting, data transfer, logistical support, etc.)	

Technical Autonomy Index

The challenges to evaluate technical autonomy lay in the unavailability of specific data for all countries. This required setting an analytic framework wide enough to encompass data available for all actors, and still specific enough to allow for a useful comparison.

Areas	Entries	Elements considered
Production phase	Generic technologies	Autonomy in terms of components, microelectronics, EEEs, etc.
	Ground systems	Autonomy in production for the specific hardware and underlying technologies
	Launch systems	Autonomy in production for the specific hardware and underlying technologies
	Satellite systems	Autonomy in production for the specific hardware and underlying technologies
	Modules, capsules and probes	Autonomy in production for the specific hardware and underlying technologies
Operational phase	Launch	Autonomy in launching any payload, of any desired weight, to any desired orbit, considering available launchers and launch sites (human spaceflight excluded)
	Orbit operations	Autonomy in operating spacecraft, including collision avoidance, rendezvous, orbital raising, disposal or re-entry, with clear relevance of TT&C and SSA
	Crewed activities	Autonomy in training and launching astronauts, as well as conducting human operations in orbit, with relevance of TT&C
Exploitation phase	Data acquisition and management	Autonomy in accessing and managing various types of satellite data, with the clear relevance of satellite variety
	Service creation and provision	Autonomy in creating and providing satellite-based services across the satellite applications spectrum

Political Autonomy Index

Political autonomy has been evaluated according to qualitative elements thought to be those necessary for a country to be domestically independent and agile, as well as free from foreign interests and resilient from external pressures in space-related decision-making.

Areas	Entries	Elements considered	
Internal sovereignty	De jure and de facto power to define interests and policies on its own	Clarity and effectiveness of the attribution of competences and powers to implement space-related decisions	
	Executive autonomy	Level of effectiveness in taking and implementing space-related decisions	
	Robustness to interference from constituents and concurrent interests	Capacity of decision/policy-makers to persuade various national interests, subordinate them and align them to national goals	
	Preference for autonomous solutions	Level of preference for local solutions over foreign ones (national launchers, suppliers, contractors, service providers, etc.)	
External sovereignty	Decision making autonomy from foreign interests	Degree of freedom of national decision-makers legislating and implementing policies etc. without accepting externally dictated authority structures	
	Robustness to foreign invitations/political or diplomatic pressures	Extent to which decision-makers can act disregarding foreign pressures and the adoption of invitations, voluntary policies that compromise the autonomy of their own polity	
	Endurance to foreign restrictions/interventions	Extent to which a nation, including its commercial actors, is affected by foreign restrictions, regulatory measures and actions (e.g. ITAR)	

References

Al-Rodhan, N. R. (2012). *Meta-geopolitics of outer space*. London: Palgrave Macmillan.

Dolman, E. C. (2001). *Astropolitik: Classical geopolitics in the space age*. London: Frank Cass Publishers.

Fox, J. G. (2001). Some principles on space strategy (or 'Corbett in orbit'). *Space Policy* (17), 7–11.

France, M. E. (2000). Back to the future: Space power theory and A. T. Mahan. *Space Policy* (16), 237–241.

Fredriksson, B. E. (2006). *Globalness—Toward a space power theory*. Montgomery: Air University Press.

Gray, C. S. (1996). The influence of space power upon history. *Comparative Strategy, 15*(4), 293–308.

Gray, C. S., & Sheldon, J. B. (1999). Space power and the revolution in military affairs: A glass half full? *Airpower Journal, 13*(3), 22–38.

Harter, M. E. (2006). Ten propositions regarding space power: The dawn of a space force. *Air and Space Power Journal, 20*(2), 64–78.

Havercroft, J., & Duvall, R. (2009). Critical astropolitics: The geopolitics of space control and the transformation of state sovereignty. In N. Bormann & M. Sheehan, *Securing outer space* (pp. 42–58). Routledge.

Hyatt, J. L., Paul, L. L., Rampino, M. A., Ricchi, R. R., & Schwarz, J. H. (1995). *Space power 2010*. Montgomery: Air University Press.

Johnson, D. J., Pace, S., & Gabbard, B. (1998). *Space: Emerging options for national power*. Santa Monica: RAND Corporation.

Joint Chiefs of Staff. (2002). *Joint doctrine for space operations*. Washington, DC: Joint Chiefs of Staff. Retrieved from Joint Chiefs of Staff.

Jusell, J. J. (1998). *Space power theory: A rising star*. Montgomery: Air University Press.

Kepron, M., Hitchens, T., & Katz-Hyman, M. (2011). Preserving freedom of action in space: Realizing the potential and limits of U.S. spacepower. In C. D. Lutes & P. L. Hays, *Toward a theory of spacepower—Selected essays* (p. 391). Washington, DC: National Defense University.

Klein, J. J. (2006). *Space warfare: Strategy, principles and policy*. Abingdon: Routledge.

Logsdon, J. M. (2001). Just sat wait to space power. *Issues in Science and Technology, 17*(3), 33–36.

Lupton, D. E. (1988). *On space warfare: A space power doctrine*. Montgomery: Air University Press.

Lutes, C. D. (2008, April). Spacepower in the 21st century. *Joint Force Quarterly* (49), 66–72.

Oberg, J. E. (1999). *Space power theory*. Colorado Springs: U.S. Air Force Academy.

Peter, N. (2009, April). Space power and Europe in the 21st century. *ESPI Perspectives*.

Swilley, S. F. (2011). *Space power: A theory for sustaining US security through the information age*. Leavenworth: School of Advanced Military Studies.

U.S. Air Force. (1998). *Air force doctrine document 2-2*. Montgomery: Air Force Doctrine Center.

Wagner, J. W. (2005). *Spacepower theory: Lessons from the masters*. Montgomery: Air University Press.

The manufacturer's authorised representative in the EU is Springer Nature Customer Service Centre GmbH, Europaplatz 3, 69115 Heidelberg, Germany. If you have any concerns regarding our products, please contact ProductSafety@springernature.com

Printed and bound by CPI Group (UK) Ltd, Croydon, CR0 4YY
30/09/2026
02225468-0014